The Struggle over Black Lives Matter and All Lives Matter

Rhetoric, Race, and Religion

Series Editor: Andre E. Johnson, University of Memphis

This series will provide space for emerging, junior, or senior scholars engaged in research that studies rhetoric from a race or religion perspective. This will include studies contributing to our understanding of how rhetoric helps shape race and/or religion and how race and/or religion shapes rhetoric. In this series, scholars seek to examine phenomenon from either a historical or contemporary perspective. Moreover, we are interested in how race and religion discourse function rhetorically.

Recent Titles in This Series

The Struggle over Black Lives Matter and All Lives Matter, By Amanda Nell Edgar and Andre E. Johnson

Desegregation and the Rhetorical Fight for African American Citizenship Rights, By Sally F. Paulson

Contemporary Christian Culture: Messages, Missions, and Dilemmas, Edited by Omotayo Banjo Adesagba and Kesha Morant Williams

The Motif of Hope in African-American Preaching during Slavery and the Post–Civil War Era, By Wayne E. Croft, Sr.

The Womanist Preacher: Proclaiming Womanist Rhetoric from the Pulpit, By Kimberly P. Johnson

Women Bishops and Rhetorics of Shalom: A Whole Peace, By Leland G. Spencer

What Movies Teach about Race: Exceptionalism, Erasure, and Entitlement, By Roslyn M. Satchel

The Struggle over Black Lives Matter and All Lives Matter

By Amanda Nell Edgar and Andre E. Johnson

LEXINGTON BOOKS
Lanham • Boulder • New York • London

Published by Lexington Books
An imprint of The Rowman & Littlefield Publishing Group, Inc.
4501 Forbes Boulevard, Suite 200, Lanham, Maryland 20706
www.rowman.com

6 Tinworth Street, London SE11 5AL

British Library Cataloguing in Publication Information Available

Library of Congress Cataloging-in-Publication Data Available

ISBN 978-1-4985-7205-7 (cloth : alk. paper)
ISBN 978-1-4985-7206-4 (electronic)
ISBN 978-1-4985-7207-1 (pbk. : alk. paper)

♾™ The paper used in this publication meets the minimum requirements of American National Standard for Information Sciences Permanence of Paper for Printed Library Materials, ANSI/NISO Z39.48-1992.

Printed in the United States of America

We dedicate this book to the many activists who stand in the rich tradition of protest trying to make this country and world a better place.

Contents

Acknowledgments

Like social justice organizing itself, writing a book about the participants in a dynamic social movement like Black Lives Matter and its countermovement in #AllLivesMatter demands investment from a lot of people. We argue in this book that a movement is its people, and we owe the ideas in this book to the people who supported them, encouraged them, and shared them with us. First and most, we thank the participants who engaged with us and each other openly and in good faith. The perspectives given freely by movement and countermovement affiliates were gifts, and we were honored to spend the time and community with those whose views are represented in this book.

The task of gathering participants together was greatly aided by the support of Daphene McFerren and the Benjamin L. Hooks Institute for Social Change at the University of Memphis. Without your generous support, this book would not exist. We also thank the Department of Communication at the University of Memphis, particularly Sandy Sarkela and Craig Stewart, for the financial and intellectual support necessary to complete this project. The top notch work our research assistants contributed to this project made it feasible; thank you to Kelly Ford, Bradly Knox, Alice Reid, and Cameron Brown for your work in support of this project. Our departmental writing group, "The Juniors," kept us accountable: many thanks to Christi Moss, Michael Steudeman, Sachiko Terui, Lori Stallings, and David Goodman.

We are grateful for Nicolette Amstutz's work as our editor, and the anonymous reviewers who offered quality feedback both on the full manuscript and through various conferences to which we submitted along the way. Early versions of this work were presented at NCA, SSCA, RSA, and SCoR. Feedback at these venues was instrumental in shaping the ideas in this book, and we are particularly grateful to Lisa Corrigan and conference respondents for offering substantive and generative feedback in these presentations.

On a personal note, Amanda would like to thank Aaron Dechant for his unwavering belief in this project and to shout out to all of the family and friends who have patiently listened to her pontificate over the politics and (mis)framings of BLM and #ALM for the past three and a half years: Melissa Click, Jamie Kern, Holly Holladay, Sara Trask, Mallory Raugewitz, Mom, Dad, Andi, Milo, Raptor, Anekin, Kate, and Roxie. She is also so grateful to Andre Johnson for sharing his wisdom, unmatched work ethic, and friendship with her.

Andre would like to thank his wife and partner, Lisa, for her insight, wisdom, and activism. Also, he would like to thank his Gifts of Life Ministries church family for allowing him to write, research, protest, and still serve as pastor. Finally, he would like to thank Amanda Nell Edgar for sharing her vision and inviting him to join her in researching BLM and #ALM. He is a much better scholar by serving as her research partner and co-author of this book.

Introduction

A Movement from the Margins

In the weeks and months following the murder of seventeen-year-old Trayvon Martin at the hands of neighborhood watch vigilante George Zimmerman, social media was awash with posts both demanding justice and blaming the victim for his own death. Alongside these raw emotional reactions to Martin's murder and Zimmerman's subsequent acquittal, hashtags like #Justice4Trayvon and #HoodiesUp demonstrated the power of Black Twitter to rally around injustice and quickly spread the word about anti-Black violence through social media. This cultural moment also demonstrated the tendency for Black organizing to be met with examples of the same anti-Blackness activists seek to combat. As Charlton McIlwain, Deen Freelon, and Meredith Clark write in their 2016 report, social media users supporting Zimmerman and suggesting Martin deserved to die for his "threatening" appearance added noise to the online conversation.[1]

The volume and variety of posts surrounding Zimmerman's trial is perhaps the reason the first Black Lives Matter (hereafter BLM) Facebook post and subsequent tweet went largely unnoticed. However, when another teenager, Mike Brown, was gunned down by white police officer Darren Wilson in the St. Louis suburb where he lived, social justice Twitter was ready. This time, BLM was not only noticed, but instrumental in helping those in Ferguson to spread the word about what was happening on the ground. Then as the grand jury deliberated on whether to indict Wilson, and when their decision not to seek further justice for Brown was released, the hashtag became a massive phenomenon. As McIlwain, Freelon, and Clark note, the BLM hashtag had only been used forty-eight times prior to the month Brown was killed. That month, the hashtag was used fifty-two thousand times, increasing to ten thousand posts in the first twenty hours following the announcement that Wilson would not be indicted for Brown's murder.[2] Here, too, many social media users were eager to counter BLM's message, and in that same timeframe, Google searches for All Lives Matter (hereafter #ALM) increased sevenfold.[3] These discourses quickly proliferated, growing into a tangle of ideas difficult to discern from any single standpoint.

As difficult as it was to make sense of the discourses surrounding BLM and #ALM,[4] journalists and cultural critics did their best to categorize the conflict. *The Guardian* called BLM "the birth of a new civil rights movement,"[5] while 1960s civil rights activist Barbara Reynolds wrote "it's hard for me to get behind Black Lives Matter" in *The Washington Post*.[6] Writing for *The Huffington Post*, Jesse Damiani attempted to get readers' attention by declaring "every time you say 'all lives matter' you are being an accidental racist," even while supporters of #ALM included a host of celebrities of color, including Jennifer Lopez, rapper Fetty Wap, singers Christina Milian and Keke Palmer, and *TLC*'s Rozonda "Chilli" Thomas. No post was above controversy. Both #ALM and BLM had supporters and opposition, which only complicated the situation. Not only were people posting in support of BLM and #ALM, now they were also disparaging the opposition by co-opting the other hashtag. As Kitsy Dixon and many in the initial wave of Twitter "Big Data" researchers remind us, it is difficult to determine the context and subtleties of an individual tweet, particularly where things like sarcasm and mockery are involved.[7] At this point, neither #ALM nor BLM were easily deciphered through numbers alone.

This book argues that untangling the struggle over BLM and #ALM requires a closer look at the ways the past emerges through individual engagement, including historical and local, everyday, lived contexts. In the midst of moments of resistance, both to systemic marginalization and to the messages that illuminate oppression, individuals often struggle to make sense of larger patterns of conflict and community. Often, we turn to statistics and trends, mapping out the ways broad demographic categories like race and gender are imagined to neatly predict political allegiance. *The Struggle over Black Lives Matter and All Lives Matter* offers a different view. Instead of moving from publicly distributed social media posts to explanations of cultural dynamics, we ask individuals to account for their own behaviors. We centralize the agency of BLM and #ALM affiliates to explain their own motivations, thus mapping these moments of resistance from their foundation: the individual participant. Working from conversations with these users, we argue that even when movement participants are not actively considering history, the culture created by previous civil rights movements and their respondents inform BLM and #ALM affiliates' behaviors and motivations through a lens of individual experiences and ideologies. *The Struggle over Black Lives Matter and All Lives Matter* calls social movement scholars and analysts to put an ear to the ground, listening for the ways local histories and experiences reverberate through social media networks.

MEMPHIS: FORGING A
CONTINUED (BLACK) RESISTANCE

According to historians Aram Goudsouzian and Charles McKinney, during the nineteenth century Memphis "became the most populated—most vibrant—metropolitan area for black people in the entire Mid-South region."[8] This led to the creation of many Black institutions that took on the "task of reshaping the city—and the nation—to better conform to the principles of equality."[9] For instance, in the aftermath of what scholars now call the Memphis Massacre, African Americans not only took the risk of providing testimony against the perpetrators of the violence, but Black Memphians banded together to rebuild what white terrorists destroyed.[10] After the 1917 lynching of Ell Persons by a mob of five thousand white people,[11] Black Memphians banded together and spoke out against the atrocity. According to historian Darrius Young, in resistance to the Persons lynching, many Black Memphians rejected military enlistment, mobilized serious efforts to vote, and plugged in to national civil rights platforms to channel the power of these organizations against lynching and other forms of white terrorism in Memphis.[12] These efforts also led to the formation of a branch of the NAACP. The civil rights institution granted Memphis its own chapter on June 26 of the same year Persons was murdered, and the chapter "played an integral role in expanding the NAACP's presence in the South."[13]

Into the mid-twentieth century, Black Memphis resistance continued to organize and protest the injustices the city's powerful white elite directed toward them. Often city officials, led by the powerful and corrupt E. H. (Boss) Crump's political machine, openly attempted to suppress any type of activism or demonstration. In the fall of 1940, for instance, law enforcement conducted a sustained campaign of harassment including illegal searches and seizures, mass arrests, and violence. Dubbed by the Black newspaper, the *Chicago Defender*, the "Reign of Terror," police occupation of Beale Street and Black neighborhoods throughout the city lasted from October to December in 1940.[14] Spearheaded by an interracial group comprised of clergy and educators speaking out against the Crump machine's tactics and aided by the investigation into activities of police by the Justice Department, the Reign of Terror finally ended. However, it also exposed rifts and sowed discord within the Black community. As Jason Jordan notes, following the Reign of Terror, "whenever certain Black Memphians opposed the draconian measures of the Crump regime, Crump no longer had to send in his troops as he had in the fall of 1940. Some of the fiercest opponents of so-called Black agitators in Memphis were other Black Memphians."[15]

Many Crump loyalists found themselves out of favor following the politician's death in 1954. A new group of middle-class African Americans started to oppose discrimination and systematic oppression in Memphis. The major

goal was to end segregation throughout the city. The changes to racial political and economic structures in the era following *Brown vs. Board of Education* propelled some Black Memphians into the middle class and positions of
leadership in the early 1960s. The city's Black youth leveraged this context
to organize around continued inequality and injustice, achieving some important gains in the city's racial structures.[16] However, Shirletta J. Kinchen
reminds us that after successfully challenging the segregation ordinances in
the city, Black Memphians were still faced with several hurdles in structural
inequality as well as the cultural backlash following the city's racial restruc-
turing.[17] For instance, many young people still encountered daily harassment
and brutality from the police, and many still lived in impoverished communities.[18] Many young people and budding activists placed the blame on the
NAACP's use of coalition politics to avoid the violent uprisings and unrest
that happened in other southern cities. According to Kinchen, "Since many
of the middle-class leaders negotiated with whites, that caused some in the
black community to believe that their decisions were being made in the best
interest of the city's black elite first and the community second."[19] For
younger Black Memphians, this recalled the days of "Boss Crump," suggesting the need for an organization independent of "traditional black leadership." Frustrated with the way things were going, these younger Black activists formed groups that would eventually give rise to the Black Power
movement in Memphis.[20]

It was these groups, namely the Black Organizational Project and the
Invaders, that began to organize disaffected groups of Black people in Memphis. After the death of Martin Luther King Jr. in 1968, these grassroots
organizations started to take matters into their own hands. No longer waiting
for the Black middle class to lead, these groups started informational campaigns, after-school programs, and book clubs aimed at instilling pride and
unity in the Black community. They operated under the belief that if people
took more pride in themselves, it would translate to better engagement from
the people in their communities. This pride eventually would reach the cam-
puses of both LeMoyne-Owen College and Memphis State University as
Black students started to protest about unfair conditions at their schools.[21]
Although these newer groups would promote and proclaim the tenants of
Black Power, they also considered themselves part of the ongoing civil rights
movement, and for their trouble, they were harassed and brutalized by law
enforcement and surveilled by both the Memphis Police Department and the
FBI. In writing about one of these groups, the Invaders, Kinchen notes,
"fascination, curiosity and disgust encapsulated the way many Memphians
viewed the Invaders" and "many both black and white branded the youth as
trouble."[22] Despite calls from a few others to take a closer look at these
young people and hear what they had to say, many simply ignored those
pleas. The way that many treated Memphis civil rights organizations, includ-

ing those grounded in Black Power advocacy and the middle-class Black city leadership, reverberates today in responses to shouts and posts of "Black Lives Matter!"

PARTICIPATORY CRITICAL RHETORIC FOR ONLINE/OFFLINE SOCIAL MOVEMENTS

Motivations for both the advocacy of BLM and the resistance of #ALM are rooted in the history of civil rights organizing in Memphis and beyond. However, though all messages bear the markings of history, they also shift depending on the personal political commitments of those who share them. In the case of BLM and #ALM, the majority of social media posters did not write longform think pieces, deliver public lectures, or publish in academic journals; they only posted on social media. What they posted was widely available, but *why* they posted was largely left to imagination and assumption. Most people knew these hashtags were widespread. In the case of BLM, we knew local movement chapters were cropping up across the country. We could make educated, hopefully historically informed, guesses about the goals of these posts. Yet without speaking to users, it was difficult to determine why, how, and with what emotional investments these online and offline messages were spreading. Did posters feel empowered by these tags? Did they believe they were part of a movement? How did they communicate with others about BLM and #ALM offline? What did they hope the tags would accomplish? Why had they been drawn to post these ideas in the first place? We believed these questions were crucial to understanding the everyday experience of social movements in the age of the internet, and we believed the only way to find answers was to speak with people directly.

Much of the previous literature on social movement rhetoric has focused either on social movement leaders, largely in offline historical contexts, or online digital communication. In the case of BLM, though, we were compelled by the clear crossover between online posting and on-the-ground movement organization. Certainly, social media has broken new ground for social movement organizing, led not only by BLM but also by posters involved in movements like Occupy Wall Street and the Arab Spring, among others. Still these movements demonstrate not only the promise of social media for spreading awareness, but also the inherent link between online social justice investments and experiences in offline culture.

Representing both a new mechanism of social movement organizing and the echoes of previous cultural norms, social media offers only one piece of the larger cultural patterns that contain it. Axel Bruns and Jean E. Burgess point out that Twitter, heralded by many as the political tool of the twenty-first century, represents only a single piece of public discourse.[23] Within this

fragment of conversation, users have the freedom to limit what they encounter; hashtags not only facilitate quick access to topics of interest, they also
contribute to a distorted sense of overall public discourse.[24] While our offline
connections, with friends, family, coworkers, neighbors, and others in our
community, seem to fade away in a digital world, Jeffrey S. Juris notes, these
connections actually limit the types of messages we encounter through social
media.[25] Lived physical experiences therefore hover in the background, less
visible but no less relevant to our experience of public opinion and political
culture.

Not only do offline connections matter in the digital space of social media, cultural structures of privilege and oppression follow users from the
physical world into the digital. Recalling the early and optimistic days of the
Internet, Lisa Nakamura and Peter Chow-White dispel the idea that digital
media identities could be neutral and anonymous.[26] Like the larger cultural
structure, they note, "the Internet and other computer-based technologies are
complex topographies of power and privilege."[27] Race remains a salient
aspect of online communication, since users carry their performances of
racial identity into both their communication strategies and their evaluation
of others' messages.[28] As Heather Hensman Kettrey and Whitney Nicole
Laster note, "Users typically perform online identities in a manner that mirrors their off-line identities."[29] To imagine that online communication would
be uninfluenced by larger cultural structures is to imagine that deeply held
connections with historical and contemporary power relations would somehow dissipate when users sat down with their computers or phones, a utopian
but unlikely situation.

Just as social media performances are reflections of offline identities and
behaviors, online participation in social movements connects with on-the-
ground investments, albeit in messy and unpredictable ways. Juris points out
that social movements that focus our attention on the use of Twitter and
Facebook are never entirely based in those media; instead social media offers
a way of connecting various offline networks together in a way that eases
organization.[30] 1960s civil rights leaders used Wide Area Telephone Service
(WATS) lines to reach out to members of the movement, but this process was
somewhat tedious.[31] One of social media's primary contributions to social
movement organizing, then, is the ability to reach large numbers of people,
many of whom are already connected to one another as friends and family.
This does not mean, though, that these movement members could not have
been reached otherwise. Many Tahrir Square protesters were recruited in
person not online,[32] and #Occupy's on-the-ground mass communication
methods were in many ways as innovative as its social media use.[33] Most
social media networks also include offline interaction, either as the impetus
for the social media connection or through ongoing, regular interaction.

Understanding the rhetoric of contemporary social movements requires that method and approach mirror the complexity of the relationship between social media and traditional on-the-ground social movements. While traditional rhetorical sources like speeches are as relevant today as in previous generations of scholarship, these texts miss the crucial work of social media in contemporary justice work. Likewise, though much rich data is available through Twitter, social media is only one small piece in the overall schema of large-scale social change. Therefore, as John Postill and Sarah Pink argue, scholars should focus not on "internet ethnography" but on "internet (related) ethnography" that draws attention to the connections between offline and social media networks.[34] By applying a lens that foregrounds motivations and experiences of ordinary social media participants, we can more fully appreciate the ways online and offline communities inform one another. Such an approach acknowledges the problems of separating communities into online and on-the-ground, more fully embracing the messy overlaps that blur the two.

To this end, we approached our study of Memphis BLM and the #ALM countermovement through a lens of participatory critical rhetoric, bringing together our training in traditional and contemporary rhetoric and audience ethnography. Michael Middleton, Aaron Hess, Danielle Endres, and Samantha Senda-Cook define participatory critical rhetoric as "a set of research practices that bring qualitative methods of data collection such as participant observation, interviewing, and oral history into the process of doing rhetorical criticism."[35] In the case of *The Struggle over Black Lives Matter and All Lives Matter*, one author's qualitative experience lies primarily through training in audience ethnography, a method that prioritizes the ideologically informed interpretations of television and other media audiences, while the other brings experience in rhetoric, race, religion, and community organizing to the process of documenting the experiences of BLM and #ALM in Memphis.[36]

With funding from the Benjamin L. Hooks Institute for Social Change at the University of Memphis, we began recruiting participants in March 2016. We recruited both through social media and word of mouth, seeking participants who were at least eighteen-years old, who had posted on social media (broadly defined) about either BLM or #ALM, and who were willing and able to come to the University of Memphis campus for a sixty-to-ninety-minute interview. We experienced no difficulty recruiting BLM advocates, likely in part because the BLM Memphis chapter was regularly meeting, and our participants were happy to spread the word about our interviews. On the other hand, recruiting #ALM participants was a struggle, despite the $20 compensation offered for participating in an interview. This may be due to #ALM supporters distrusting our motives, but we also noticed that, although think pieces continued to circulate disparaging #ALM, public use of the hashtag on social media in our region had all but vanished by this point. In fact, the last few #ALM posts on Twitter in our area mocked the hashtag rather than supporting it, making recruitment there difficult. Most of our BLM recruitment occurred through Facebook, Twitter, and word of mouth, while our most successful #ALM recruitment efforts came through sites like Craigslist, Nextdoor, and an email listserv serving a cluster of middle-class neighborhoods.

In all, we spoke with forty-six participants, twenty-nine who affiliated with BLM and seventeen who affiliated with #ALM.[37] Prior to the interview, participants completed a questionnaire containing demographic questions as well as several Likert and open-ended questions about recent social media posts and conversations with others about BLM or #ALM. The demographic portion of the questionnaires revealed that our participants were 63 percent women and 72 percent Black or African American with an average age of thirty-seven.[38] Though we expected the majority of our #ALM supporters to be white, this was not the case; rather, #ALM-affiliated participants were only slightly whiter than the general demographics of the greater Memphis area at 41 percent. In other words, 59 percent were Black or African American. The median family income for our participants, both across and within the BLM and #ALM groups, was $25,000 to $50,000. This is representative of Memphis' median family income of $46,873 per year. Our participants also represented educational levels from high school diplomas to graduate degrees, and a variety of social media use from one to four regularly used platforms (e.g., Twitter, Instagram, YouTube, Facebook, etc.).

During interviews, we asked participants about the messages they had seen and shared about BLM and #ALM, their conversations about the hashtags, and what they understood BLM and #ALM to represent, both independently and in relationship to the other hashtag. In these interviews, we aimed for a very conversational and relaxed feel. We believe we accomplished this, based on feedback from participants, many of whom have reached out to us in the years since the interviews. As Frank (Black, 37, Pastor) remarked toward the end of his interview, "I just really hope that, in the publication of this, that they really find a way to transpose that we were really hand clapping and stuff (laughter from Frank and the group). . . . The joy involved in this, the solidarity involved in this, the affirmation of everybody's humanity."[39] All BLM interviews were conducted in groups like the one Frank discussed. Most #ALM participants were more comfortable speaking one-on-one, with eleven interviews conducted privately, but the responses and gratitude for the opportunity to share their thoughts were similar. It was clear in these interviews that people had a lot to say and were hungry for opportunities to share. Audience studies research tells us that different people will approach media in different ways, and that, as Katherine Sender points out, the idea of a singular audience united by monolithic usage and understanding of particular media is largely a market-driven and scholarly made myth.[40] We do not claim that our participants represent all users of BLM and #ALM. Yet the intimacy with which participants spoke to us about their investment in BLM and #ALM demonstrates the importance of speaking with social media users beyond simply looking at their posts online, and it illustrates the value of reaching out to actual movement participants beyond gathering the perspectives of leaders.

In all, we spoke with participants for just over twenty-one hours. This resulted in 664 single-spaced transcribed pages, which we coded following Anselm Strauss's process of open coding.[41] This allowed us to ground our findings "in data on the page as well as on the conjunctive experiential data," including our knowledge of the city's political and socio-historical context.[42] In the following chapters, we will break down our analysis to demonstrate individual group patterns, largely discussing responses from BLM and #ALM participants separately. The relationship between these groups is messy, though, and much less predictable than we (and most think piece authors) predicted prior to this study. To provide a broader context for the discussions we had with BLM and #ALM posters, in the following section, we offer an overview of the quantitative feedback from the questionnaires we administered prior to interviewing participants. We believe these statistical results demonstrate some broad similarities and difference between and within groups.

SHARED IDENTITIES AND
SOCIAL MEDIA AGREEMENT

One of this book's key contributions is an exploration of how investments in various identities influenced participants' views of social justice affiliation and efficacy. The importance of demographics was not surprising in our participants' survey responses; the two primary axes of identity that influenced perceptions were race and class. First, participants who identified as either Black or African American were more likely to believe people in their social media networks agreed with their views on BLM than were our white participants. That race would play a pivotal role in discussions of BLM and #ALM is perhaps not surprising, though, as we will detail in chapter 2, race often did not predict which group affiliation participants claimed.[43] As we will discuss in chapter 1, those who identified with BLM often discussed issues of racial injustice both online and in their conversations with friends and family. Additionally, as we will discuss in chapter 5, BLM participants often self-censored their more controversial views for fear of retribution. While they shared their ideas with others, they did so cautiously, and more often when they were certain others would agree with their views.

Second, for those with annual family incomes at or below $50,000, the sense that the majority of their social media networks agreed with their views on BLM was weaker than their wealthier counterparts.[44] It bears mention that $50,000 per year in income is slightly higher than the Memphis median family income of $46,873. Yet among those with this solidly working-class income level, the sense of support from online social networks was weaker. In other words, working-class participants felt less certain that others in their online networks agreed with them. We suspect this can be explained by the additional axes of oppression imposed by lower income, such that less financially secure participants also felt less secure in having the world on their side. Those with higher incomes, on the other hand, would enjoy more freedom to distance themselves from others, through unfriending or unfollowing, particularly among co-workers. Certainly, our participants were aware of the potential for affiliation to impact their career opportunities, as we discuss in chapter 5.

We asked participants to tell us how strongly they believed others in their social media feeds agreed with their stances on BLM and #ALM, as well as how strongly they believed others in the United States in general agreed with them. Across BLM and #ALM groups, the more someone believed their social media network agreed with their views on BLM and #ALM, the more they believed the majority of the country agreed with their views on BLM and #ALM.[45] This finding supports the robust work on political polarization through social media, indicating that, at least within our participant pool, social media users whose networks agree with their views are likely to overestimate the extent to which others in general support their positions.[46] As Benjamin R. Warner has argued, the more we cull our social media feeds to think and look more like us, the more pronounced this effect is likely to be.[47] This type of polarization is harmful to democracy, as the belief that all reasonable people agree with your particular stance often forecloses the possibility of conversation.

When we compared our BLM and #ALM groups,[48] we found that #ALM affiliates believed more strongly that most people in America agreed with their views than those who affiliated with BLM.[49] In other words, #ALM affiliates answered with significantly more confidence that others agreed with their stances. This finding raises questions about how polarization might influence not only our perception that others agree with us but also how different groups interpret this agreement. It stands to reason that those who feel certain that their beliefs are in the majority will be more difficult to persuade. Yet given the evidence of a relationship between social media networks and perceptions of the country in general, perhaps hashtags like BLM could work as an intervention into a larger sense of national belonging *through* social media. Put simply, a change in social media might open a space for an offline persuasion.

Taken together, these aspects of identity and social media perception frame a call for the revival of Martin Luther King's Poor People's Campaign of 1967 and 1968. Perhaps not coincidentally, King characterized Memphis's sanitation workers' strike as an enactment of both the issues driving the Poor People's Campaign and a demonstration of the ways protest could address these injustices.[50] Though our findings point specifically to participants' perceptions of social media solidarity, they also highlight the ways race and class, though aligned by histories of social injustice, have come to be perceived as at odds with one another. Particularly in the lead up to the 2016 presidential election, the time we were surveying and interviewing participants, the idea that the non-Black poor and working class could and should be in alignment with the goals of BLM became increasingly difficult to find on the national political stage. As we discuss later in this book, the racial division between BLM and #ALM is less clear than many had previously assumed. By centering the context and motivation for BLM and #ALM involvement, we focus on both the similarities and differences between and within these groups, aiming to illustrate the possibilities and background knowledge that make coalition possible.

BOOK OVERVIEW

While scholars and cultural critics have explored Black Power and civil rights social movements since the 1960s, studies of emerging rhetorics like BLM are less developed, particularly in terms of the tension that emerges from the #ALM backlash. We take this controversy as a new opportunity to explore racial advocacy, as opposed to the class- and gender-based organizing that are often the focus of online social movement literature. This book addresses this issue by illuminating the performances and motivations of the BLM movement and #ALM advocates, and the ways these enactments travel between online and offline communities. We argue that context must be central to how both groups are understood, since the BLM movement and the #ALM countermovement draw from both changes and stagnations in American culture. While many have argued that #ALM is simply the racist backlash against BLM, we propose a more nuanced explanation for the motivations and practices of these two groups' online and offline communication to reveal the similarities and differences in how they understand one another and the United States in general. By focusing on cultural influences, including the history of Black liberation rhetoric, contemporary postracialism, the politics of fear, and religious discourses, we intervene in debates about both contemporary racial justice rhetoric and traditional, text-based rhetorical inquiry, offering a lens of contextualized motivations to move both discussions forward.

The first chapter outlines the ways BLM participants define the emergence and meaning of the BLM movement. We first offer a historical overview of the rhetoric of Black social movements and how that rhetoric finds resonance within the contemporary Memphis movement. Drawing from this lens, we discuss ways in which participants understood BLM as well as their place within the movement. While our participants articulated many of the traditional Black liberation rhetorics, they also wrestled with how to articulate those expressions to a wider audience. Despite the common refrain of many BLM activists that "this is not your grandparents' movement," or "I am not my grandparents, you can catch these hands," participants' articulations of contemporary Black liberation organizing mirrored those of the 1960s civil rights movement.

Building from the previous chapter, chapter 2 outlines the ways #ALM participants define the countermovement in relationship to BLM. We first offer a historical overview of counter- and anti-movement rhetoric as well as an overview of the concept of white fragility, often discussed in debates about #ALM. Working through this lens, we then discuss the ways our #ALM participants understood the countermovement. While our participants articulated many of the contours of traditional understandings of countermovements, they differed from traditional discussions of countermovement history in the way they oriented themselves in relation to the status quo. Rather than reinvesting in the direction of the status quo, #ALM participants understood their countermovement as working toward social change, but in a more constructive manner than BLM. This distinction was marked by concerns about segregation and conflict between citizens, so that, while white fragility was not absent from their discussions of #ALM, they more often sought protection for others they understood as incapable of discussing race, rather than for themselves.

Chapter 3 focuses on participants' use of religious narratives. Here, we examine the rhetoric of these narratives to explore how participants' faith, religion, or spirituality led them to support BLM both online and "out in the streets." Though BLM is a secular movement, this does not mean that participants are "nonreligious" or "antireligious." Indeed, the three women who coined the phrase Black Lives Matter consider themselves religious, albeit not in traditionally Christian ways. For many participants, the movement has "inspired and energized Black Christians" in Black churches.

The fourth chapter offers the converging contexts of postracialism and a culture of fear as a framework for understanding many of our #ALM advocates' motivations. For our participants, fear was a primary motivation for #ALM support, as they understood the world as increasingly dangerous. Since these fears were fragmented, participants sought a concrete object of blame. While most participants believed in core aspects of BLM's mission, particularly in terms of countering violence and helping those who suffer, they rejected a framework that centralized race. Employing a postracialist lens, participants read BLM's focus on race as discursive violence, leading them to resist the movement even while ostensibly supporting its goals.

In chapter 5, we offer the relationship between real life and digital identities as a context that limits the possibilities for translating participants' motivations to their rhetorical behaviors. Put simply, our conversations with BLM advocates reveal that the kinds of surveillance that attempted to block racial justice organizing during the civil rights movements have shifted inward, creating powerful self-surveillance mechanisms that prevent discussions of race in contemporary culture through fears of damage to relationships, career trajectories, and personal emotional health. These same fears were adopted by #ALM affiliates, which obfuscated the ways censorship blocks social change rather than simply creating discomfort among social groups. Through a rhetorical analysis of these emerging themes, we build on previous arguments about the silencing of racial justice discourse to argue that the threat of outside repercussions can lead people to self-censor online conversations about race and racial justice advocacy.

Finally, we conclude by revisiting the major themes, goals, and implications of this book. Here, we argue that without attention to both context and motivation, the national and scholarly conversation surrounding racial justice rhetoric is incomplete. We therefore urge readers to consider the influences of various contexts on performances of BLM and #ALM, both taking seriously the things that draw people into these rhetorics and acknowledging the unequal consideration mainstream culture grants to the motivations and performances of marginalized communities. In these final remarks, we summarize our process of placing context and motivation in conversation with one another, arguing that these factors should ground our understanding of social justice rhetoric.

By tracing the everyday experiences of BLM and #ALM in Memphis, *The Struggle over Black Lives Matter and All Lives Matter* records the BLM movement and the #ALM response as a moment in cultural history. We hope that this approach promotes contemporary racial justice movements like BLM by contributing to the growing body of literature on this movements' importance, while simultaneously demonstrating the value of speaking with people involved in social movements and documenting their ideas in the moment. By putting contexts in conversation with motivations, *The Struggle over Black Lives Matter and All Lives Matter* demonstrates one way of considering racial justice movements in the digital age.

NOTES

1. Charlton McIlwain, Deen Freelon, and Meredith Clark, "Beyond the Hashtags: #Ferguson, #Blacklivesmatter, and the Online Struggle for Offline Justice," *Center for Media and*

Social Impact, February 29, 2016, http://cmsimpact.org/resource/beyond-hashtags-ferguson-Blacklivesmatter-online-struggle-offline-justice/.

2. Ibid.

3. According to a Google Trends search for All Lives Matter. Note that the Google search was originally for the three words together rather than the hashtag. https://trends.google.com/trends/explore?date=2014–11–01%202014–12–01&q=All%20lives%20matter.

4. We use BLM to denote Black Lives Matter and #ALM to denote #AllLivesMatter. The absence of the hashtag for BLM nods to the on-the-ground work of BLM chapters across the country. Conversely, #ALM is organized as a countermovement only in online spaces. However, we did not change the syntax of participants' references, which occasionally referenced BLM as a hashtag or #ALM as a movement or more general offline culture.

5. Elizabeth Day, "#BlackLivesMatter: The Birth of a New Civil Rights Movement," *The Guardian*, July 19, 2015, https://www.theguardian.com/world/2015/jul/19/Blacklivesmatter-birth-civil-rights-movement.

6. Barbara Reynolds, "I Was a Civil Rights Activist in the 1960s. But It's Hard for Me to Get behind Black Lives Matter," *Washington Post*, August 24, 2015, https://www.washingtonpost.com/posteverything/wp/2015/08/24/i-was-a-civil-rights-activist-in-the-1960s-but-its-hard-for-me-to-get-behind-Black-lives-matter/?utm_term=.8b9fb3b49d3f.

7. Kitsy Dixon, "Feminist Online Identity: Analyzing the Presence of Hashtag Feminism," *Journal of Arts and Humanities* 3, no. 7 (2014): 34–40.

8. Aram Goudsouzian and Charles W. McKinney, Jr., "Introduction," in Aram Goudsouzian and Charles W. McKinney, Jr., (eds.), *An Unseen Light: Black Struggles for Freedom in Memphis, Tennessee* (Lexington, KY: University Press of Kentucky, 2018), p. 4.

9. Ibid., 4.

10. The Memphis Massacre happened from May 1–3, 1866. A congressional committee investigated the massacre and concluded that forty-six Black people died, 285 people were injured, over one hundred houses and other property belonging to African Americans were burned. Though no one was ever convicted of the crimes, scholars credit the testimony from the Black people affected by the terror and the continued determination of Blacks to build community that led to Tennessee ratifying the Thirteenth and Fourteenth amendments to the constitution. For a more detailed history of the Memphis Massacre see, Stephen V. Ash, *Massacre in Memphis: The Race Riot That Shook the Nation One Year after the Civil War* (New York: Hill and Wang, 2013).

11. On May 22, 1917, a white mob took Persons from custody and lynched him. After they lynched him, they dismembered him and threw his head at a group of African Americans on Beale Street.

12. Darrius Young, "The Saving of Black America's Body and White America's Soul: The Lynching of Ell Persons and the Rise of Black Activism in Memphis," in Aram Goudsouzian and Charles W. McKinney, Jr., (eds.), *An Unseen Light: Black Struggles for Freedom in Memphis, Tennessee* (Lexington, KY: University Press of Kentucky, 2018), p. 49.

13. Ibid., 52.

14. Jason Jordan, "We'll Have No Race Trouble Here: Racial Politics and Memphis' Reign of Terror," in Aram Goudsouzian and Charles W. McKinney, Jr., (eds.), *An Unseen Light: Black Struggles for Freedom in Memphis, Tennessee* (Lexington, KY: University Press of Kentucky, 2018).

15. Ibid., 145–46.

16. Shirletta J. Kinchen, *Black Power in the Bluff City: African American Youth and Student Activism in Memphis, 1965–1975* (Knoxville: University of Tennessee Press, 2016), p. 13.

17. Ibid.

18. Ibid., 36.

19. Ibid., 41.

20. Ibid., 43.

21. Kinchen, *Black Power in the Bluff City*.

22. Ibid., 114.

23. Axel Bruns and Jean Burgess, "The Use of Twitter Hashtags in the Formation of Ad Hoc Publics," Paper presented at the European Consortium for Political Research conference, Reykjavik (August 25–27, 2011).

24. Yarimar Bonilla and Jonathan Rosa, "#Ferguson: Digital Protest, Hashtag Ethnography, and the Racial Politics of Social Media in the United States," *American Ethnologist* 42, no. 1 (2015): 4–17.

25. Jeffrey S. Juris, "Reflections on #Occupy Everywhere: Social Media, Public Space, and Emerging Logics of Aggregation," *American Ethnologist* 39, no. 2 (2012): 259–79.

26. Lisa Nakamura and Peter A. Chow-White, "Introduction—Race and Digital Technology: Code, the Color Line, and the Information Society," in *Race after the Internet*, ed. Lisa Nakamura and Peter A. Chow-White (New York: Routledge, 2012).

27. Ibid., 17.

28. Heather Hensman Kettrey and Whitney Nicole Laster, "Staking Territory in the 'World White Web': An Exploration of the Roles of Overt and Color-Blind Racism in Maintaining Racial Boundaries on a Popular Web Site," *Social Currents* 1, no. 3 (2014): 257–74.

29. Ibid., 259.

30. Juris, "Reflections on #Occupy Everywhere."

31. Julian Bond, interview by Elizabeth Gritter, *Southern Cultures* 12, no. 1 (2006).

32. Malcolm Gladwell, "Does Egypt Need Twitter? *New Yorker* Political Scene Blog," *New Yorker*, February 2, 2011, https://www.newyorker.com/news/news-desk/does-egypt-need-twitter.

33. Naomi Klein, "Occupy Wall Street: The Most Important Thing in the World Now," *Critical Quarterly* 54, no. 2 (2012): 1–4.

34. John Postill and Sarah Pink, "Social Media Ethnography: The Digital Researcher in a Messy Web," *Media International Australia* 145 (2012): 123–34.

35. Michael Middleton, Aaron Hess, Danielle Endres, and Samatha Senda-Cook, *Critical Participatory Rhetoric: Theoretical and Methodological Foundations for Studying Rhetoric in situ* (Lanham, MD: Lexington Books, 2015), p. xiv.

36. Amanda Lotz, "Assessing Qualitative Television Audience Research: Incorporating Feminist and Anthropological Theoretical Innovation," *Communication Theory* 10, no. 4 (2000): 447–67.

37. Eleven participants had supported both BLM and #ALM, often within the same post, but supported one or the other more strongly.

38. We identify participants' racial identifications as we discuss their responses in the following chapters. We asked for racial identification in an open-ended question and use the term listed by participants (Black or African American, for example).

39. All participant names are pseudonyms. We asked participants to choose their own pseudonyms, as we felt this would best represent their personalities and personal investments. In most cases we used the names provided by participants, though we sometimes substituted a different name to avoid confusion.

40. Katherine Sender, *The Makeover: Reality Television and Reflexive Audiences* (New York: New York University Press, 2012).

41. Anselm L. Strauss, *Qualitative Analysis for Social Scientists* (Cambridge: Cambridge University Press, 1987).

42. Ibid., 29.

43. On the question of whether participants' social media networks agreed with their stances on BLM, Black participants (M = 4.44, SD = 0.73) sensed stronger agreement than white participants (M = 3.50, SD = 1.51); $t(40) = 2.70$, $p = 0.01$.

44. There was a significant difference in the scores for perceived social media agreement between those with a family income below \$50,000 (M = 3.80, SD = 1.14) and those with a family income of \$50,000 or above (M = 4.68, SD = 0.65); $t(40) = -3.10$, $p = 0.004$.

45. There was a positive correlation between participants' sense that the United States agreed with their views and that their social media networks agreed with their views ($r = 0.459$, $n = 41$, $p = 0.003$).

46. See for example Benjamin R. Warner, "Modeling Partisan Media Effects in the 2014 U.S. Midterm Elections," *Journalism and Mass Media Quarterly* (2017).

47. Ibid.

48. Here, we removed those who supported both #ALM and BLM, which we will discuss in further detail in chapter 2.

49. There was a significant difference in the scores for perceived US agreement between BLM affiliates (M = 14.48, SD = 2.42) and #ALM affiliates (M = 17.00, SD = 3.56); $t(29) = -2.18, p = 0.038$.

50. Martin Luther King, Jr., "I've Been to the Mountaintop," April 3, 1968, *American Rhetoric*, http://www.americanrhetoric.com/speeches/mlkivebeentothemountaintop.htm.

Chapter One

"It Means I Matter"

The Emergence and Meanings of BLM

On August 24, 2015, the *Washington Post* published a scathing critique of the Black Lives Matter movement from Barbara Reynolds.[1] Criticism of BLM is not new, and with any movement that centers on fighting for social justice and standing with Black people, one expects criticism from opponents. However, Barbara Reynolds is not your typical opponent. As one who was "trained in the tradition of Martin Luther King Jr.," she would not readily oppose many of the criticisms BLM levels against systemic injustice and would support many of the initiatives that BLM offers. However, in her op-ed, she takes BLM to task. She wrote that "Black Lives Matter is a motley-looking group," that "looks, sounds and feels different" than the movement she was a part of in the 1960s. While many veterans of the civil rights movement admired the "cause and courage" of BLM protesters, they did not agree with BLM's approach. She reminded her readers that she and other activists during the 1960s were "nonviolent activists who won hearts by conveying respectability and changed laws by delivering a message of love and unity." She argued that "BLM seems intent on rejecting our proven methods. This movement is ignoring what our history has taught."

She continued in her op-ed to tell of how her generation of activists "confronted white mobs and police brutality with dignity and decorum," and that sometimes they would dress in church clothes and kneel in prayer during protests to "make a clear distinction between who was evil and who was good." For Reynolds, this notion of faith and spirituality served them well.

> The 1960s movement also had an innate respectability because our leaders often were heads of the Black church, as well. Unfortunately, church and

spirituality are not high priorities for Black Lives Matter, and the ethics of love, forgiveness, and reconciliation that empowered Black leaders such as King and Nelson Mandela in their successful quests to win over their oppressors are missing from this movement. The loving, nonviolent approach is what wins allies and mollifies enemies. But what we have seen come out of Black Lives Matter is rage and anger—justifiable emotions, but questionable strategy. For months, it seemed that BLM hadn't thought beyond that raw emotion, hadn't questioned where it would all lead.

While we take issue with her argument that "church and spirituality are not high priorities in Black Lives Matter" in chapter 3, throughout her widely read essay, Reynolds condemned BLM for distancing themselves from their elders and not "seizing the wisdom of veteran civil rights activists." The group, she argued, lacks "discipline, respect for elders, [and] restraint," all of which she suggested were "badly needed in the movement." For Reynolds, BLM represents the stereotypes of irresponsibility and naivete manifested in a group of "young activists."

A primary strategy Reynolds uses to demonstrate BLM's supposed immaturity is through accusations that they lack a "clear strategy" or "well-defined goals," a common theme among the editorials disparaging the movement. To support her argument, Reynolds quotes Oprah Winfrey. Winfrey, in an interview promoting her then-upcoming film *Selma*, remarked:

> I think it's wonderful to march and to protest and it's wonderful to see all across the country, people doing it. But it's not enough to march. What I'm looking for is some kind of leadership to come out of this to say, "This is what we want. This is what has to change, and these are the steps that we need to take to make these changes, and this is what we're willing to do to get it." I think what can be gleaned from our film, is to take note of the strategic, peaceful intention required when you want real change.[2]

The critique that BLM activists do not have any goals or plans beyond protesting or that many in the movement do not know what BLM even means is a familiar one. Beyond Reynolds and Winfrey, many others have offered this same line of critique. Contrasting BLM against the civil rights movement of the 1960s, for example, Andrew Young bemoans the contemporary movement's tactics, arguing:

> In our movement, we were not only spiritual, we were thoughtful. The reason our campaigns for change were successful in Montgomery and Birmingham was because they were undergirded by boycotts. We didn't burn any businesses down. I don't see that discipline here. We also trained people not to get angry because we knew our minds, not our emotions, were our most powerful weapons. We knew—to lose your wits was to lose your life.[3]

Former chairwoman of the Black Panther Party Elaine Brown, too, offered critiques of BLM in her widely shared interview with *Spiked* magazine.[4] When asked how the Black Panther Party compares with BLM, she responded, "I don't know what Black Lives Matter does, so I can't tell you how it compares to what the Black Panther Party was . . . I don't know what Black Lives Matter does. So, if you can tell me, I'll give you my thoughts." Echoing Andrew Young's accusation that BLM lacked discipline, she continued:

> There is no comparison. The next wave of young people running out here, who are complaining and protesting about the murders of young Black men and women by the police all over the country, they will protest, but they will not rise up in an organized fashion, with an agenda, to create revolutionary change. We advocated community self-defense organizations to be formed so that we would not be assaulted by the police, so that we would bear arms and assume our human rights.[5]

Editorials like these continued to appear in social media feeds, apparently demonstrating that the movement was, according to *CNN*'s John Blake, "all over the place. Four years after its founding, BLM is still a movement without a clear meaning for many Americans."[6] Yet across these articles, the most glaring lack was not discipline, goals, or organization; what these editorials lacked was the voices of BLM's membership.

In this chapter, we outline the ways BLM affiliates define the emergence and meaning of the BLM movement. We first offer a historical overview of the rhetoric of *misremembering* Black social movements and how that rhetoric finds resonance within the Memphis movement. Drawing from this lens, we discuss ways in which participants understood BLM as well as their place within the movement. While our participants articulated many of the traditional Black liberation rhetorics, they also wrestled with how to articulate those expressions to a wider audience. Our findings showed that despite the common refrain of many BLM activists "this is not your grandparents' movement," or "I am not my grandparents, you can catch these hands," participants understood and articulated their movement in their own times similarly as those in past Black liberation movements.

THE MISREMEMBERING OF THE MOVEMENT

That both civil rights movement veterans and current BLM activists tend to misremember past Black liberation movements is not surprising because many others do as well.[7] Kirt Wilson reminds us, "Our collective civil rights memory affects how we discuss our civic and social interests in the present."[8] As the groundwork for contemporary conversations, including those that shape our political futures, this public memory is crucial to civic discourse. Though it is "always partial and incomplete," Wilson argues, "it has real political and material effects."[9] The 1960s civil rights movement, in particular, represents a fraught and contested space of history. Not only do contemporary social justice organizations use various pieces of the mid-twentieth century movement as a blueprint for organizing, as Randall Kennedy points out, conservatives today "celebrate and exaggerate the gains of the movement precisely to reverse progress."[10] With various factions articulating history in particular ways and to specific ends, the lessons of the civil rights movement can be understandably difficult to trace.

In seeking those lessons, particular players often get lost, reflecting the rhetorical patterns of mass public memory. As Randall asserts, there are those who seek to "domesticate the movement, homogenize it, make it universally palatable."[11] He further writes that these people "delete from the movement's history its troublesome radical outcroppings, subordinate its communal character to tales of individual heroism, and make the narrative into a story of American triumphalism."[12] While this approach allows conservative groups to leverage the political disruption of the civil rights movement for their own ends, such tactics are not limited to those on the political right. In fact, Reynolds and the other critics replicate this pattern in their critiques of BLM. In comparing the civil rights movement to BLM, they tend to "domesticate the movement" to make it palatable for current use. As they live in their nostalgic rhetorical constructions, they delete all of the suffering, pain, and problems that were also part of the movement. Neither is the strategy of domestication limited to one generation. Contemporary activist Rahiel Tesfarmariam, in her op-ed in the *Washington Post*, suggests that leaders of the Ferguson and Baltimore uprisings "changed the predominant image of Black activism in America."[13] She writes:

> The front lines of the fight for civil rights are no longer "manned" by the traditional leaders of the Black community: well-dressed, respectable clergymen. . . . Today's movement has dismissed these criteria, operating without centralized leadership and accepting as many straight women and LGBTQ people on the front lines as straight men. . . . For this generation, there's no need to hide behind a veil of purity or wear a suit to have an authoritative seat at the table. This is a movement that encourages all to "come as you are." Natural. Bohemian. Rebellious. Tatted up. Provocative. Ratchet. It seems everything is acceptable—except the constraining rules of our elders' day.

In Tesfarmariam's retelling, the civil rights movement was characterized by "nonviolent resistance strategies," while the movement for Black Lives has been more "confrontational." As evidence, she cites that demonstrators have "disrupted morning commutes, theatrical performances, and athletic events." In doing so, she also misremembers the strategies of disruption employed throughout the mid-twentieth-century movement. Tesfarmariam's contemporary, Brandon Dixon, put it this way:

> For BLM organizers, the docility shown by Civil Rights activists is too weak to address the nation's race problems. For Civil Rights activists, nonaggressive tactics were necessary to highlight the often egregious racism and prejudice of the institutions oppressing African Americans. BLM believes that the nature of the current world—a faux color-blind society that is ignoring rather than addressing racism—is not conducive to the same approach. In their eyes, it needs a jarring blow to encourage its leaders to change. That unabashed approach makes people uncomfortable, especially in a society that has ebbed closer and closer to a state where the extreme of political correctness is the new norm.[14]

Common to these retellings is a polarizing narrative that pits "nonaggressive tactics" against "jarring blows," peaceful protest against violence, and ultimately a perception of respectability against effective political disruption.

While we are sympathetic to the "histories" that both civil rights veterans and BLM advocates assert, these are misreadings of the history of the movement. For instance, while Reynolds claims that BLM is "motley-looking group," that "looks, sounds and feels different," that perception of difference is belied by the often disparaging remarks about Reynolds's contemporaries in the 1960s. She may not agree with the BLM approach, but she seems to forget that many did not agree with the civil rights movement approaches either. Despite her contention that their message was about "love and unity," many thought that King and others were spreading messages of disunity and hate.[15] For all the talk about "dignity and decorum," these did little to protect the many activists who were beaten, hit, stomped, kicked, bitten, shot, and killed in their church clothes.[16] The domestication of public memory of the civil rights movement leads many to believe that the young people of Reynolds's generation had it all together, effortlessly banding together with foresight and harmony. Contrary to Winfrey's contention and seamless depictions of organizing in the film *Selma*, mid-twentieth-century movement activists did not always have a plan, they did not always get along, and they did not always know what they were going to do next.

The domestication of the civil rights movement has consequences beyond the bad-faith leveraging of public memory and external criticisms of BLM. By misremembering the struggles of mid-twentieth-century activists, 1960s and contemporary movement leaders and participants are robbed of the opportunity to build community and learn from one another. As Simone Sebastian writes,

> As much as BLM's opponents and supporters (who insist that "this ain't yo mama's civil rights movement") differentiate it from the 1960s effort, these two historical moments have a lot in common. Both have been op-

posed by more than half of Americans, both have needed violent confronta-
tions to attract national media attention, and both have been criticized for their
combative tactics. Whether in the 1960s or the 2010s, the aggressive disruption of American race relations has caused the same anger and fear—from
Northerners and Southerners, from Blacks and whites, from liberal "allies" and
racist adversaries. [17]

While Reynolds and others do themselves no favors by distancing their
historical approaches from those of the contemporary BLM struggle, there
are lessons and encouragements to be gathered from more accurately remembering the experiences of the civil rights movement. In particular, the historical truth of anti-Black racism, both individual and systemic, should undergird
and connect BLM and 1960s movement participants. As the *New York Times*
editorial board made clear,

> The "Black Lives Matter" movement focuses on the fact that Black citizens
> have long been far more likely than whites to die at the hands of the police,
> and is of a piece with this history. Demonstrators who chant the phrase are
> making the same declaration that voting rights and civil rights activists made a
> half-century ago. They are not asserting that Black lives are more precious
> than white lives. They are underlining an indisputable fact—that the lives of
> Black citizens in this country historically have not mattered, and have been
> discounted and devalued. [18]

When we consider "The Truth of 'Black Lives Matter,'" to borrow the
Times article title, BLM and the civil rights movement have more in common
than not.

While maybe for many Americans BLM is a movement without any clear
meaning, for advocates and activists in the movement, BLM not only has
meaning but also has mission and purpose. To activists, BLM is a social
movement with a thoroughly researched agenda coupled with plans and programs outlining the way forward. In a context filled with so much misremembering, it is perhaps unsurprising that BLM activists often articulate its
movement in stark contrast to the civil rights movement. However, the actions they take and the reflections they make demonstrate an understanding
of Black liberation eerily similar to past movements.

MEANINGS OF BLM

Created in 2012 by Alicia Garza, Opal Tometi, and Patrisse Khan-Cullors
after the acquittal of George Zimmerman and becoming more pronounced
during the events in Ferguson, BLM grounds itself in the "experiences of
Black people who actively resist de-humanization."[19] While definitions may
vary by regional and local goals, BLM's national online platform defines the

movement in terms of both policy and ideals, striving to highlight and dismantle anti-Black racism and white supremacy and the ways these systems target Black lives. As they elaborate, BLM "is an affirmation of Black folks' humanity, [their] contributions to this society, and [their] resilience in the face of deadly oppression."[20] For Julius Bailey and David J. Leonard, BLM is "first and foremost a challenge to the affront of racial violence and prejudiced policing." It is also a "challenge to white privilege and supremacy, and it seeks to disrupt the *status quo* by forcing America to unflinchingly examine the ways in which state-sponsored agents treat Black Americans as, at best, second-class citizens."[21] Further they maintain that "by spotlighting the persistent violence, and through elucidating the fallacies, hypocrisies, and double standards that anchor white supremacy," BLM challenges the "very foundations upon which Americans claim their democracy is built: that we are all created equal, that all are equally entitled to life, liberty, and the pursuit of happiness."[22]

Key to BLM's platform is the conceptualization of structural violence as far-reaching and broadly applied. Though the BLM hashtag is often used to highlight incidents of violence and murder at the hands of police, as an organization, BLM is interested in addressing all structural inequalities as mutually reinforcing and interconnected systems of injustice. Pointing out the issues of anti-Black racism that reach beyond police brutality, Xhercis Mendez writes that BLM's concerns "also include prisons, food security, anti-immigrant policy, transphobia, the assault on disabled community members, unequal access to health care and education, wage disparities, and reproductive justice for women of color."[23] Beyond these specific areas of focus, Glenn Mackin argues, BLM also demonstrates a counter-hegemonic political project through its very demonstration of agency through protest. He argues that BLM "develops a mode of political-aesthetic transformation that is fully imbricated into the sensory order that it negates. The activists enact modes of freedom and equality that the dominant order of sense denies— above all, the freedom to engage in practices in which one steps outside of one's assigned roles and reconfigures the sensory world."[24] Through demonstrations of disruption, in other words, BLM offers a sensory vision that envisions justice through the challenge of traditional hierarchical roles.

As Sarah J. Jackson notes, while the "Black lives matter movement can be traced to the legacy of the larger Black freedom movement," it also finds its home in the work of Black Millennial groups.[25] For Jackson, this has lead BLM to respond to injustices with "discourse and tactics both familiar and unfamiliar to members of the old guard."[26] Jackson notes that millennial activists reject much of the "respectability politics" of the 1950s and 1960s and have turned to "new technologies" that nurture a "counterpublic community that centers the voices of those most often at the margins."[27] As the movement grew, that "counterpublic community," as Lebron reminds us, "cannot be identified with any single leader or small group of leaders, despite the role Khan-Cullors, Tometi, and Garza played in giving us the social movement hashtag. Rather "#BlackLivesMatter represents an ideal that motivates, mobilizes, and informs the actions and programs of many local branches of the movement."[28] It's broad approach to racial justice means that the brand is easily transferable to local or regional groups invested in the fight against structural anti-Black racism.

Our study demonstrates that most of our respondents shared these definitions and understandings of BLM. Respondents' definitions of BLM centered on "affirmations," "being human," and "resistance." They define BLM following Bailey and Leonard, in identifying the movement as a challenge to status quo oppressions.[29] They expand the meaning of BLM, as Mendez reminds us, to other issues and concerns germane to African Americans and all of society, while, as Jackson notes, seeing and defining themselves as nurturing a counterpublic that centers the voices of those on the margins.[30] In short, our participants' knowledge of the "herstory" of BLM helped them define what it means personally to them. When asked to define BLM, the definition they crafted also helped to define their own role in the movement, reflecting the importance of personal connection as a motivation for movement participation. Thus, the overwhelming majority of our respondents did, in fact, see BLM, as Lebron described, as a "social movement brand that can be picked up and deployed by any interested group of activists inclined to speak out and act against racial injustice,"[31] particularly when that deployment helped individuals to express their identities, interests, and experiences.

AFFIRMING LIFE IN THE MIDST OF A FIGHT

Despite those who doubted BLM members' thoughtfulness or dedication to movement participation, our respondents were very well versed on BLM. When asked directly, "What does BLM mean to you?" many participants had several answers speaking to the ways the movement connected with various areas of their personal histories. Often participants framed their explanation of BLM in terms of the meanings of humanity, emphasizing that the movement was about declaring the value of a whole person, particularly in the face of dehumanizing social systems. For example, Ganda (African American, 35, Student/Research Assistant) explained that BLM means "life." She elaborated, "It means life—not just us here existing—[but] us being able to live, access to good food, clean water, these are the things that living beings have. That's what Black Lives Matter means to me." She also added that BLM means "getting to a point where we can accept ourselves and be happy with ourselves and be prideful in ourselves." Ganda's explanation demonstrates the ways participants understood the aspect of "lives" as central to BLM, not only in terms of living, but also of living with dignity and respect.

Martin (Black, 43, Activist) reiterated Ganda's explanation, rooting his definition of BLM in a quote that he attributed to Malcolm X: "We declare the right to be a human being, to be respected by, and by any means necessary, we have to fight for these rights." He sees BLM as a call to "fight for the voiceless. The ones that have been silenced due to the intersection of other identities—gender, sexuality, classism, and things and so forth. So, for me, to sum it up, it means life here in America—to fight for justice and equality." Martin's definition of BLM also punctuated his understanding of the goals and objectives of the movement. He told us that the number one goal of BLM was to stop police brutality in all forms. However, he did not stop there. He then included the goals of quality education, health, equality, and accountability, punctuating his understanding of the movement with the need for a fully conceptualized understanding of humanity.

When placed in this context, the movement's focus on oppressive social systems connect deeply to expressions of both pain and love. For instance, Martha (White, 30, Minister) said that "Black Lives Matter is an outcry from people and communities who have been oppressed and made marginalized. It's a voice for that." Tom (Irish American, 37, Student/Teacher/Minister) told us that for him, "Black Lives Matter is a movement that responds to injustices, specifically against African American lives." Chanel (Black, 28, Nonprofit Program Coordinator) grounded her definition of BLM to a "flawed justice system." Taylor (Black, 20, Student) said that for her BLM meant simply "stop killing us because we matter." Sue (African/Indian, 52, Stylist) placed the meaning of BLM within a historical context. She said when she thinks about the meaning of BLM she thinks about

> "I am a man," because I think more in terms of we're human, first. Um, so it made me go to, "Black people are human." It doesn't have to be any kind of special treatment. Um, it's just if you see everyone as a human, you'll be kinder. You'll try to be more inclusive. You'll try to understand them even if they have a different perspective because you say, "Well, I'm a human." So that's what it hit for me and, um, I have a son so, you know, it's real important for me. But, I always go back to him as we're people first. No matter what your religion is, your race, your, you know, if you have straight hair, curly hair; whatever it is, you're a human first. You were born.

In each of these cases, participants articulated the pain of marginalization through a lens of a humanity. They spoke out against violence not only from a defense of bodies' right to live but also from the perspective of full human beings.

Connecting BLM to deeply held understandings of what it means to be a whole person made participants' responses intensely intimate. BLM, for them, meant considering the pain of marginalization within the context of access to dignity and respect. Angela (Black, 37, Musician/Activist) located the meaning of BLM within the context of her surroundings and of her own agency.

> Well, with me when I say, or when I hear Black Lives Matter; it means I matter. You know, and it's not so much I'm saying, "I matter," it's a response to everything that had taken place all the way back to before my ancestors came over here. Our entire culture and generation was taken from another country and brought here, and to this day we still do not get the same treatment, dogs get treated better. As a matter of fact, right here in the city of Memphis, the grass is more important at Overton Park than a Black person. Not to take anything away from that movement but you've got people upset at folks with Black Lives Matter signs and T-shirts, and hashtags. So, when Black Lives Matter is said, I say, "I matter," and not to say that you don't matter; but understand that I am just as important as you, if not anybody else.

Angela's discussion nods to protests that had happened surrounding the possibility of paving over the "greensward," a stretch of grassy land adjacent to the Memphis Zoo. For Angela, these protests seemed to elicit more empathy from white Memphians than did the lives of her fellow Black citizens. That Angela's points were rooted in her everyday experiences of living in Memphis and America were underscored by her posting habits. Highlighting the importance of living as a whole person, and as speaking her truth from her own position in the world as a musician and activist, Angela shared that her most recent post on BLM was a video of the Black Eyed Peas' song "Where Is the Love." Angela, like other participants we spoke with, was drawn to participate in BLM by her sense of the ways the movement spoke to things she already felt deeply connected to. Living and loving as a whole person led participants to fight for dignity, respect, and humanity, as articulated through their everyday lived experiences.

REPRESENTATION AND HUMAN DIGNITY

In articulating the ways BLM spoke to everyday experiences and expressions of dignity, participants often shared specific examples that spoke to injustices they saw around them. RBG (Black, 45, Sales) framed his understanding of all Black lives to the death of Trayvon Martin. In talking about Martin's death at the hands of George Zimmerman, he felt as if this was a "better case" to examine the "whole idea of Black Lives Matter." In his reasoning, he said that the "person who killed him was not a law official or anybody . . . [he] was just a dude. Just some random dude that killed a random child. The way that everybody treated Trayvon as far as the victim, it was kind of like the way you treat people when you're covering for the police. But Zimmerman is not a police officer, you know? . . . It wasn't totally new but it was, it was a fresh one for this day and age. You know." For RBG, media coverage of Martin's murder was particularly eye-opening in terms of the ways white media scrutinizes Black death as well as the ways that media is consumed and circulated by others.

On one hand, the community rallied around the death of Trayvon Martin even though Zimmerman was not a police officer. By saying this, RBG lifts two important reminders. First, even though defenders of Zimmerman framed him as a "law enforcement officer," he was not. He was just some "random dude" out that night. The story of him being the Neighborhood Watch Coordinator did not give him any license or authority as a law enforcement officer. Second, the death of Trayvon Martin also demonstrates that from the outset, BLM has been about all Black lives and not only the ones at the hands of law enforcement officers. What RBG reminds us in his definition of BLM is that the movement started as a response to a "random dude" with no state-sponsored authority, killing a "random child" who was just trying to get back home to watch the second half of the NBA All-Star Game. For him, BLM helped him and others to stand up and let people know that "we ain't gon' take this."

On the other hand, RBG was disturbed by the ways media coverage of the Martin murder followed in the long tradition of framing Black victims as somehow the perpetrators of their own deaths. Speaking to the tendency for journalists to feature negative images of Black victims and neutral or positive images of their murderers, RBG continued,

> Every time you kill one of us off, you're now finna go get this picture with him throwing up a finger sign [or] something and just paint this negative picture of him. He's, he's, and now you go up pull up a 13-year-old record when he broke a window. And you just paint this whole picture, you know . . . he gets killed, they go find his old records, broke a window when he was eight. Drunk a beer: he's an alcoholic. You know, just paint this whole picture of him. You know what I'm saying, and then this other [white] kid gets killed: "He was a Christian boy. He was just led wrong." They might paint a picture wrong of his parents, but he's gonna be scot-free and just. . . . He was broken. Somebody should've gave him a hug. It's like, if they both matter, then why, why didn't [the Black child] need a hug too?

RBG's description points to the importance of addressing both literal violence and symbolic indignities, illustrating the ways these issues work together to undergird a white supremacist society. That unfair treatment of Black people by white systems was further reaching than physical violence was common to how our participants discussed BLM. This was the case when Blair (African American, 21, Student) gave a comprehensive definition of BLM. For her, BLM meant focusing on "all the injustices that Black people face within the justice system or white supremacy," a prospect that reached beyond physical violence to also counter unfair treatment in a range of institutions. Similarly, April saw BLM as raising issues of representation across rhetorical contexts. As she explained, BLM means that Black people have "some sense of self-worth and self-esteem." Central to the movement, for April, was that BLM's messaging is "about human dignity that all people need to come to understand."

Central to the articulation of equal human dignity was fair treatment across the board. Artemis (White, 23, Unemployed) emphasized the importance of recognition in social systems. She argued that BLM means "you deserve to be acknowledged and that you want to be acknowledged and that everyone deserves to be acknowledged," highlighting as others did that BLM was about the interaction of representational equality with physical state violence. In response to her comment about acknowledgment, and the vocal agreement it encouraged in the room, we asked who should acknowledge the marginalized. One respondent answered "everyone" while Artemis answered "society." Then she expounded on her point, noting "if I go and drive down the street in a really nice car, they're not going to pull me over for some random reason, but if a Black guy does it, there's a good chance." Artemis's answer illustrates the interaction of representation with unequal treatment under the law. Her answer addresses the disparity between her likely privilege as a white woman, even though she was in our lowest income bracket, and that of a Black man. For her, then, BLM was about addressing differential treatment by the law and recognizing that disparities like the one she described are created and encouraged by representational politics. While our participants did not often explicitly connect these dots, the politics of seeking out a negative picture of Trayvon Martin explicitly feeds the racist stereotypes that lead to police harassment of people of color. This theme, then, underscored the ways our participants saw BLM, as the synergy of representation and law often underscored comments.

Media representation offers a straightforward and common mode of engagement for potential group members. By linking together something well-known to the participant with something they may be less certain about, representational politics allows potential BLM members to safely try out a place in the movement. At the time of her interview, April's most recent post, for example, included the BLM hashtag along with a story about Piers Morgan's comments about Beyoncé's *Lemonade*. Though the story did not relate explicitly to BLM, it offered a rebuttal to Morgan's comments that he preferred the singer to be "less inflammatory [and] agitating."[32] The article April shared challenged the idea that political engagement was beyond the scope of appropriate commentary for Beyoncé. That this connected with the missing of BLM for April demonstrates the relationship between representation, dignity, and politics that explicitly sanction violence against Black people. At the same time, posting about Beyoncé or other popular culture topics can feel safer to participants than overt and explicit political commentary. Here, as in other cases, a connection to personal identity, experience, and expression is key to engagement with social movements like BLM.

ALL BLACK LIVES MATTER

Reflecting recent conversations in many online circles about the importance of intersectionality, many of our participants insisted that "all Black Lives Matter." This understanding squares directly with the founders' intentions of BLM, which expressly centralize the intersecting axes of oppression at work in systemic anti-Black racism. The national BLM website is careful to emphasize inclusivity, noting that coalition-building is more successful in spaces that welcome and recognize many identities and experiences. Recognizing those who are often left out of racial justice conversations, BLM explicitly uplifts "Black queer and trans folks, disabled folks, undocumented folks, folks with records, women, and all Black lives along the gender spectrum."[33] In other words, BLM is intentional about advocating for all Black lives.

This focus on inclusivity was clear to our participants, though it highlighted some tension at times. For many, the intersection of race and gender, regardless of performance, was central to their experience and understanding of a new Black liberation movement. Stella (Black, 37, Student/Homemaker) grounds her definition with the understanding that all Black lives matter. She explained,

> Of course, as a Black woman, it covers all aspects of Blackness. Black lives matter whether you're a woman, whether you're a man, whether you fall into the category of young, upcoming . . . , student, whatever it happens to be. We seem to . . . get tossed into these categories, so which lives matter even in the Black lives? Now, so to me, it means what it says. It says Black lives matter too because historically Black lives have not mattered and we're trying to make people aware of how much so. So it's all Black lives, whether you're sagging, swagging, it doesn't matter what degree to which you are Black or your representation of Blackness. All Black lives matter.

This clarification is key for Stella, and other participants, because they recognize that true inclusivity and intersectionality is difficult to achieve and has often been neglected in previous social movements, Black and otherwise. Following this, Rashaun (African American, 22, Student) wondered if BLM, for some, meant only a "particular group of people." Taking note of this, Stella added that BLM is an "effort to be inclusive. It's an effort to be fully inclusive because, again you have the gay, lesbian, transgender. You have the whole community, and it started from, just to be a little, be more honest, from that place of the furthest reach. Where the people who would normally be excluded when you a woman and you gay." Here, Stella articulates a key argument of Kimberle Crenshaw's intersectionality: if social justice organizations centralize those who are disadvantaged by multiple axes of oppression, everyone in the movement will benefit.[34]

Crenshaw's call for social justice organizations to more clearly attune themselves to the needs of their most vulnerable members follows a long tradition of self-reflexivity among social movements and those who study them. Demonstrating this tactic, Frank (Black, 37, Pastor) offered some nuance to the understanding of "all Black lives." Frank shared that when he uses "all Black lives matter that is primarily a response to the respectability politics that exist within the Black cyberspace or even the Black psyche more broadly. So when I use all Black lives matter, I'm primarily talking to Black people and if white people are eavesdropping then so be it." Further, he said:

> Black lives matter today in April of 2016 references not just the ideology or the psychology of Black dignity and value and worth but also the network that has been associated with the founders of the Black Lives Matter movement; the three queer sisters who spearheaded the effort in response to the Trayvon Martin murder. So I would like to differentiate between that, the usage of that for me. When I'm saying Black lives matter I'm talking to everybody. When I say all Black lives matter I'm primarily talking to Black folks.

This shift in audience speaks to the care our participants took in thinking through issues of BLM. In considering Frank's call for introspection within his community, it is clear he and others we spoke with did not display the type of immature, feckless attitude of which BLM members are often accused. Instead, Frank and others' comments reflect the ways motivation speaks to an interior self: since BLM members are often driven to participate by their own identities and experiences, their interpretations of the movement are deeply personal. In this way, the everyday practices of BLM often reflect the investments of its members.

These investments are not uniformly intersectional, and some participants struggled with the ways BLM aimed to address issues they saw as separate from Black liberation. For example, Dr. Pegues (African American, 41, Engineer) struggled with the inclusive nature of BLM. After noting that she would like to see BLM be "inclusive of all nationalities," and reminding us that "Rabbis were on the bridge with Dr. King," she articulated her concerns about an "LGBT push" in the movement. After saying this, she quickly reminded us that she was "not homophobic" and that she has "friends that are gay and family members that are gay and lesbian." However, she believed that BLM was forcing the LGBT agenda "down [her] throat." Though this was not an overwhelming sentiment, the intersection with other social movements occasionally showed up as a moment of tension for participants. April (Black, 55, Minister), too, shared some hesitation about the expediency of intersectional social movements. Specifically, she felt that the 1960s civil rights movement had been "hijacked by the women's movement, hijacked by the gay and lesbian movement." Like Dr. Pegues, April expressed some inner conflict over this, noting that she was "not against progression," but she felt she had observed a "hijacking . . . of Black Lives Matter . . . in counter, to counter Black Lives Matter." Taken together, these articulations of BLM as an intersectional movement, whether participants embraced or rejected inclusivity, demonstrate the clarity with which BLM communicated its orientation to serving all Black lives. That BLM strove to be intersectional is clear from our participants. Also clear is that messages about intersectionality stir up widely circulated rhetorics of exclusivity, including, in some cases, issues of homophobia, sexism, or a rejection of particular performances of race.

HISTORY MATTERS

Many of our respondents tied their definition and understanding of BLM to an understanding of movement history. Despite the constant refrain, "this is not your grandparents' movement," many in our study understood the role history plays in shaping what activists do today. An example of this comes from Frank, who grounds his understanding of BLM in the historical oppression of Black people:

> For me, generically speaking, Black Lives Matter is a response to the historical oppression and exploitation of Black people, Black bodies and the dehumanization of Blackness. And so Black Lives Matter is not just a response, it's also the affirmation, it's a verbal, symbolic, rhetorical affirmation of the value, the dignity, the humanity of Black people and Blackness.

By rooting his discussion in the historical disregard for Black lives, Frank brings together the issues others had raised in their discussion of humanity, dignity, and the whole person. Affirming Frank's sentiment but centering the fact that "Black lives" traditionally have not mattered at all in America, Thurman (Black, 55, Minister/Adjunct Professor), on the other hand, illustrated the role of history in BLM through a story. He shared,

> I remember having a conversation with my father and him talking about him growing up in rural North Carolina where there were Black people that were killed with impunity. I mean, you'd just . . . it was another Black person gone, and nothing was done to correct that or even attempt to bring people to justice. And, if they did have a trial, it was over in five minutes, and the, the people who were involved were, you know, not guilty, and it was almost a joke even to have that. And then, even in cases where his mother was killed, and there

never was even an attempt to have an investigation or anything. It was just another Black person, another Black life lost. It's really to bring to the fore-front the fact that, um, Black lives do matter, but in a lot of quarters and in a lot of situations, it hasn't always, and then, um, helping people to, to be aware of that and start to correct some of those wrongs.

This deeply personal remembrance, in which Thurman recounts Black history through his family's history, reflects two important aspects of BLM. First, at fifty-five-years old, Thurman is not the Black Millennial often ima-gined to dominate the movement, and second, iterations of history, too, speak to the importance of personal connection in the decision to participate in a social movement.

In addition to sharing his family history with the group, he also generous-ly elaborated on his memories of social movements as well as the role of popular representations in spreading discourse about BLM. Thurman remem-bered,

I grew up in an era and in a place where the Black Panthers were visible, and they were very much unlike the traditional story of being these armed radicals and things like that. They came in our school, in our classroom, they talked to us about pride. They had feeding programs. They did talk about self-protection and showed . . . because I had a fifth-grade teacher who was very sympathetic to them, so they were in our classroom all the time. And I remember on our campus in our elementary school, there was going to be a fight between two gangs and they closed school for the day and everything . . . the Panthers came and intervened and say, "Hey, this, this, this just is not it. It's not going to work. You all need to go back. This doesn't help our community." They were the ones who we saw as being advocates for the people in our town, the people of color in our town and all of that. And, so, that whole thing again, the, um, the images and things that she [Beyoncé's Super Bowl performance] brought up in that performance and the, you know, very clear connection to Black Lives Matter was an opportunity for me to have conversations with people about it again, and about the history of the Panthers as well.

That history was central to Thurman's experience, and understanding of BLM was not constant across our participants, but it often emerged as a way of understanding a personal connection with Black liberation. Len (Black, 37, Self-Employed) also shared stories that she heard growing up which gave her an appreciation of BLM.

I think the historical context and what you learn in history in schools growing up is that being different when someone exposes you to some factoid where you get to go dig into books like *A Peoples' History of the United States*, or *Sundown Towns*, or *Lies My Teacher Told Me*, and for me, um, and then hearing stories of just my ancestors and my grandparents, of things they went through, where they weren't valued . . . I got to hear those stories growing up.

It's just always been engrained that, yes you can go out before the world and do your absolute best, but you still might not matter or count in that. So, for me it just, it's something to, it's something to celebrate, it's something to make known that may not understand the context of privilege and how we exist, and it's kind of just a part of, like, every day for me.

Here Len makes explicit what was clear throughout our interviews: everyday experiences of connection drive active membership in BLM, a motivation that is particularly important when rooted in family or national history.

GOALS OF BLM

Despite the critique that proponents of BLM do not have a platform that includes goals and demands, BLM proponents continue to offer goals and demands. In short, activists believe if people do not know what those are, they have not been paying attention. One can find the clearest understanding of the goals for BLM by reading *The Vision for Black Lives.* In it, proponents of BLM list six demands and forty policy recommendations. Dani McClain, writing for the *Nation* magazine, notes that "A Vision for Black Lives" emphasizes the movement's independence from party politics and its desire to prioritize solutions that address root causes over the incremental or bipartisan proposals more likely to win a presidential candidate's support or move through an obstructionist Congress."[35] While some argue that the movement's aims are unrealistic—goals such as reparations and legislation that forces the United States to acknowledge the lasting impact of slavery—the statement "offers greater depth for readers who want to know how to translate the words into grassroots action."[36] In the platform, activists drew from earlier policy statements such as the Black Panther Party's *Ten Point* program in 1967[37] and the Black Radical Congress's *Freedom Agenda* in 1998.[38] These historical ties demonstrate the movement's understanding of and commitment to previous movements. BLM, in other words, draws not only inspiration from these movements but also information.

In asking our participants how they understood the goals of BLM, we received answers that were in line with the *Vision for Black Lives.* For example, for Laura (Black, 43, Field Organizer), one of the goals of BLM was to give the people some sense of "solidarity." Tom shared that he had learned the goals of BLM by visiting the national website to read them. In reading the goals, he knew that the movement was for him. For Angela, the goal of BLM is "Black liberation." She further explained that BLM is about liberating "us as a people where we can, not only, embrace who we are but that we can obtain things that we need. Such as social wealth. Such as job sustainability. Such as, you know, rights for the people that are coming after us. Education, different things like we want to have." This plan for liberation is clear on the national website. In fact, nearly every time we asked participants how they understood BLM's goals, someone in the group told us we could read them ourselves on the website. For participants, the goals of the movement could not be clearer.

When speaking of goals, Frank simply said that the goal of BLM was systemic change. He arrived at that answer, he told us, after the death of Sandra Bland. He told the story of how he and a friend of his recently had a conversation that centered on the arrest of Sandra Bland. He disagreed with his friend's assessment that all Bland had to do was to "comply." He argued that Bland did not break any laws when the officer arrested her and indeed was compliant with the officer's demands:

> The officer gets out of the car, asks for her license, she, A, she rolled the windows down that compliance, gets the license, that's in compliance. Was asked to sign her name on the ticket, which she signed. But, but the way that the system is structured, it's structured such that whenever there is a hitch that goes off, it has to be the victim's fault and not the system's fault. And so Black Lives Matter, especially, with its initiatives around criminal justice reform is seeking to try to change the system in such a way whereby it does not continually exploit and oppress and manipulate and even violently eradicate and exterminate Black people and Black minds.

RBG suggested that one of the goals of BLM is to help people realize that "Black Lives Matter." He sees it as "a continuation of the civil rights movement and, and more so, the Black Power movement." For him, BLM is a call to action back to the "Black Power movement," because for him, "it's Black empowerment."

When we asked Artemis the question, she divided the answer into two parts. First, she said that the overall goal of BLM was equality. Second, however, she also named some specific goals. For Artemis, one of the specific goals for BLM was "monitoring the police." She, however, did not stop there. She noted that BLM might have started with that goal, but it had since named others.

> Well, that is where it started. Um, so that's where it, it's mainly focused, but it is branching out into, you know, school equality because, you know, segregation was gotten rid of, but there's still a degree of segregation in schools because there's these neighborhoods because the poor neighborhoods are filled with, you know, Black people and the richer neighborhoods have white people, and that's not right because then the poorer neighborhoods have this really really bad school and the nicer neighborhoods have a better school, and you get this segregation that's . . . I'm not going to say it's not, it's intentional, but it's not really unintentional either.

Chanel, who identified herself as a member of the local Memphis chapter of BLM, said that

> There's a whole lot of goals that they have. One particularly that I ascribe to, I guess, being a part of the local chapter here is just justice for all people of color, Black or not, in every aspect of our lives. Economic justice, housing and environmental, and education. Justice in all facets of every part of life of a person of color. I think that's what pulls me in. This idea of doing what's right, and what we know to be is right, for all people.

Some like Ivory (Black, 23, Student/Sales Associate) defined BLM as "receiving recognition" and receiving the "same respect that others have." However, when asked about the goals, she opened up.

> The main goal of it—and in my opinion, I just feel like, we just we're tired of oppression. And when I say oppression, like, there are different forms of it at this point. And we're just sick of it. . . . And so that's what the Black Lives Matter movement is doing. We're trying to push it to make other people aware that this is an issue within our community. . . . I'm not looking for an apology from anyone, but I just want my people to be aware of what's going on. And I want us to support one another so we can—we can get to the level that they are at. Because they're not going to help us. We have to help each other. But I feel like that's one of the goals, maybe not the main goal, because we just want everybody to realize that our lives do matter just as the next person. . . . We're just ready for change. And we can't keep depending on them to do it, we have to do it. And that's what we have been doing. Not just by tweeting it, but actually putting actions behind it.

In our study, we found that the majority of our participants not only had a firm understanding of the goals of BLM, but also that those goals lined up with the platform statement in the Vision for Black Lives. For example, advocates state the reason they have created the platform, what their demands are, and the vision they cast.

> We have created this platform to articulate and support the ambitions and work of Black people. We also seek to intervene in the current political climate and assert a clear vision, particularly for those who claim to be our allies, of the world we want them to help us create. We reject false solutions and believe we can achieve a complete transformation of the current systems, which place profit over people and make it impossible for many of us to breathe. Together, we demand an end to the wars against Black people. We demand that the government repair the harms that have been done to Black communities in the form of reparations and targeted long-term investments. We also demand a defunding of the systems and institutions that criminalize and cage us. This document articulates our vision of a fundamentally different world.

Our participants not only would wholeheartedly agree with the statement above but would also attempt to put it in action.

CONCLUSION

Theon Hill writes that "memory exists in a state of constant evolution. It privileges particular ways of knowing and being while marginalizing others."[39] In this chapter, we ground the misunderstanding of some who argue that BLM activists have not defined the movement or its goals in a misremembering of past Black liberation organizing. When civil rights veterans look back fondly on their activism, they sometimes misremember how people treated and thought of them at the time. By comparing themselves to today's activists, civil rights veterans tend to cringe at some of the activities BLM promotes. Simultaneously, BLM activists often misremember the civil rights movement. As we argue in this chapter, the belief that BLM is doing something wholly new is simply false. BLM adopts many of the strategies of the civil rights movement. Despite the aggressive nature of some protests and rallies, BLM adheres to the nonviolent strategy and boycotts employed by civil rights activists. Moreover, BLM sets future agendas; they also draw upon the spirit and wealth of information from past Black liberation movements.

Despite the mutual misinterpretation, BLM advocates in our groups were deeply aware of their connection with 1960s civil rights activists. Much of their understanding of BLM and the goals of the movement first grounded themselves in their own understanding of the history of Black people in America. It was an understanding of that history as interpreted through a lens of individual identity factors including race, generational affiliation, and, as we discuss in chapter 3, faith that that propelled many to get involved in the first place. The perception of connection between some aspect of their identity and BLM's goals and messages is the basis upon which participants chose to engage. By affirming BLM, our participants connected to the past by first personally connecting with it and second, by using it to launch their own activism in their own way. In so doing, BLM helped many in our group and around the world not only to wake up but to "stay woke."

NOTES

1. Barbara Reynolds, "I Was a Civil Rights Activist in the 1960s. But It's Hard for Me to Get behind Black Lives Matter," *Washington Post*, August 24, 2015, https://www.washingtonpost.com/posteverything/wp/2015/08/24/i-was-a-civil-rights-activist-in-the-1960s-but-its-hard-for-me-to-get-behind-Black-lives-matter/.
2. "Oprah Winfrey's Comments about Recent Protests and Ferguson Spark Controversy," *People*, January 1, 2015, http://people.com/celebrity/oprah-on-recent-protests-and-ferguson.
3. Qtd. in Reynolds, "I Was a Civil Rights Activist."

4. Tom Slater, "Black Lives Matter Has a Plantation Mentality," *Spiked*, October 19, 2016, http://www.spiked-online.com/newsite/article/Black-lives-matter-has-a-plantation-mentality-elaine-brown-Black-panthers/18888#.Wrj6PS7wZhF.

5. Ibid.

6. John Blake, "Is Black Lives Matter Blowing It?" *CNN*, August 2, 2016, https://www.cnn.com/2016/07/29/us/Black-lives-matter-blowing-it/index.html.

7. For more on memory studies on the civil rights movement, see Kristen Hoerl, "Burning Mississippi into Memory? Cinematic Amnesia as a Resource for Remembering Civil Rights," *Critical Studies in Media Communication* 26, no. 1 (2009): 54–79; Christina Moss, "A Time to Remember: Rhetoric, Commemoration and Activism" in *Activism and Rhetoric: Theories and Contexts for Political Engagement*, second ed. Routledge, edited by JongHwa Lee and Seth Kahn (Forthcoming 2018).

8. Kirt Wilson, "Dreams of Union, Days of Conflict: Communicating Social Justice and Civil Rights Memory in the Age of Barack Obama," *National Communication Association*. Carroll C. Arnold Lecture, Philadelphia, 2016, 3.

9. Wilson, "Dreams of Union," 3.

10. Randall Kennedy, "The Civil Rights Movement and the Politics of Memory," *American Prospect*, May 12, 2015, http://prospect.org/article/civil-rights-movement-and-politics-memory.

11. Ibid.

12. Ibid.

13. Rahiel Tesfamariam, "Why the Modern Civil Rights Movement Keeps Religious Leaders at Arm's Length," *Washington Post*, September 18, 2015, https://www.washingtonpost.com/opinions/how-Black-activism-lost-its-religion/2015/09/18/2f56fc00-5d6b-11e5-8e9e-dce8a2a2a679_story.html?utm_term=.141dfb55b87f.

14. Brandon Dixon, "A Broken Frame: Black Lives Matter," *Harvard Political Review*, May 22, 2016, http://harvardpolitics.com/covers/48277/.

15. Rachel Tabachnick, "The John Birch Society's Anti-Civil Rights Campaign of the 1960's and Its Relevance Today," *Political Research Associates*, January 21, 2014, http://www.politicalresearch.org/2014/01/21/the-john-birch-societys-anti-civil-rights-campaign-of-the-1960s-and-its-relevance-today/#sthash.hgyzLvr5.dpbs.

16. Resistance to Civil Rights, *Equal Justice Initiative*, https://eji.org/racial-justice/resistance-civil-rights.

17. Simone Sebastian, "Don't Criticize Black Lives Matter for Provoking Violence. The Civil Rights Movement Did, Too," *Washington Post*, October 1, 2015, https://www.washingtonpost.com/posteverything/wp/2015/10/01/dont-criticize-Black-lives-matter-for-provoking-violence-the-civil-rights-movement-did-too/?utm_term=.ed2a1580eec6.

18. Editorial Board, "The Truth of 'Black Lives Matter,'" *New York Times*, September 3, 2015, https://www.nytimes.com/2015/09/04/opinion/the-truth-of-black-lives-matter.html.

19. Black Lives Matter and Alicia Garza, *Equal Justice Society*, https://equaljusticesociety.org/Blacklivesmatter/.

20. Herstory, *Black Lives Matter*, https://Blacklivesmatter.com/about/herstory/.

21. Julius Bailey and David J. Leonard, "Black Lives Matter: Post-Nihilistic Freedom Dreams," *Journal of Contemporary Rhetoric* 5, no. 3, 4 (2015): 68.

22. Ibid., 69.

23. Xhercis Mendez, "Which Black Lives Matter?" *Radical History Review* 126 (October 2016): 97.

24. Glenn Mackin, "Black Lives Matter and the Concept of the Underworld," *Philosophy and Rhetoric* 49, no. 4 (2016): 479.

25. Sarah J. Jackson, "(Re)imagining Intersectional Democracy from Black Feminism to Hashtag Activism," *Women's Studies in Communication* 39, no. 4 (2016): 375.

26. Ibid.

27. Jackson, "(Re)imagining," 375.

28. Christopher Lebron, *The Making of Black Lives Matter: A Brief History of an Idea* (New York: Oxford University Press, 2017), xi–xii.

29. Bailey and Leonard, "Black Lives Matter."

30. Mendez, "Which Black Lives Matter?"; Jackson, "(Re)imagining."

31. Lebron, *The Making of Black Lives Matter*, xii.

32. Qtd. in Taylor Pittman, "Matt McGorry Calls Out Piers Morgan's Absurd Queen Bey Critique," *Huffington Post*, April 26, 2016, https://www.huffingtonpost.com/entry/matt-mcgorry-calls-out-piers-morgans-absurd-queen-bey-critique_us_571f74f2e4b01a5ebde33e66.

33. "About," Black Lives Matter, https://Blacklivesmatter.com/about/.

34. Kimberle Crenshaw, "Demarginalizing the Intersection of Race and Sex: A Black Feminist Critique of Antidiscrimination Doctrine, Feminist Theory and Antiracist Politics," *University of Chicago Legal Forum* 1 (1989): 169.

35. Dani McClain, "What Does Black Lives Matter Want? Now Its Demands Are Clearer Than Ever," *The Nation*, August 1, 2016, https://www.thenation.com/article/what-does-Black-lives-matter-want-we-now-have-it-in-writing/.

36. McClain, "What Does Black Lives Matter Want?"

37. "The Black Panther Party's Ten-Point Program," *University of California Press Blog*, https://www.ucpress.edu/blog/25139/the-Black-panther-partys-ten-point-program/.

38. "The Black Radical Congress: A Black Freedom Agenda for the Twenty-First Century," *The Black Scholar* 28, no. 1 (1998): 71–73.

39. Theon Hill, "Sanitizing the Struggle: Barack Obama, Selma, and Civil Rights Memory," *Communication Quarterly* 65, no. 3 (2017): 355.

Chapter Two

"I'm Sorry, but You're Just Segregating Yourselves"

The Countermovement Rhetoric of #ALM

Derek's (31, Black, Teacher) first contact with #ALM did not explicitly condemn BLM, question the motives or tactics of protesters, or challenge the idea that police violence against people of color was actually a problem. The first post he remembers seeing, in fact, did not engage BLM at all. Instead, Derek described the simple picture that accompanied the hashtag as "fists in a circle, and it had different races between the fists in the circle . . . I get where they are coming from, the message from it." Explaining the salience of that image for him, particularly in a context of his multi-racial friend group, Derek told us "that one particular picture, that stuck right to me." Derek's allegiance to #ALM flies in the face of many popular assertions about the hashtag. As a Black Millennial, why did Derek feel a greater allegiance to #ALM than he felt to BLM? What led him to understand the countermovement hashtag as a symbol of unity rather than backlash? How did Derek overlook the popular discourses attaching #ALM to whiteness? Based only on popular press discussions of BLM and #ALM, the answers to these questions are elusive. #ALM's critics have not only understood the hashtag as "BLM's countermovement,"[1] but also positioned #ALM along a continuum ranging from "accidental[ly] racist"[2] to "an assertion of white supremacy"[3] comparable to segregation.

As with many controversial online discourses, the polarization of BLM and #ALM prompted a barrage of responses, which in turn added complexity to the already complicated nature of discussing race in America.[4] BLM's goals were clearly spelled out in various online locations.[5] However, given

23

the impressive diligence of BLM advocates on social media,[6] #ALM was more often defined through opposition; for many online commenters, #ALM stood for nothing except against BLM.[7] Conflicts between the two groups featured arguments about the racial make-up of police victims, inter- and intra-community violence, and respectability politics. As Eduardo Bonilla-Silva, Mark Orbe, and others note, racial ideologies are shaped and sustained through discourse.[8] In the case of #ALM, though, these discourses were not only disagreements about the meaning of race. They represented conflicting viewpoints about how we (should) talk about race, and whether discussing race in the twenty-first century is appropriate in the first place. According to much online commentary, these discourses represented the type of resistance to racial justice engagement, "in which even a minimum amount of racial stress becomes intolerable," described as white fragility.[9]

This raises the question of how to reconcile white fragility and the #ALM countermovement with the not inconsequential number of people of color who embraced #ALM and rejected BLM. Countermovement scholarship reminds us that history is peppered with these ostensibly surprising allegiances. Many women joined anti-suffrage circles, Janet Saltzman Chafetz and Anthony Gary Dworkin note, for fear of losing what little power they had negotiated within the status quo system of overt misogyny.[10] For Kristy Maddux, this situation also speaks to the propensity for other hidden factors, anti-socialist sentiment in the case of anti-suffragettes, to draw marginalized people into countermovements.[11] For many, countermovement formation may come from the desire to set the agenda for public conversation based on personal contentions about the movement or other tangentially related ideas.[12] As a result, the motivations behind engaging in a particular countermovement are varied and often more nuanced than is apparent in the broader public discourse.

Building from the previous chapter, this chapter outlines the ways #ALM participants define the countermovement in relationship to and separate from BLM. We first offer a historical overview of countermovement and counter public rhetoric as well as a discussion of the concept of white fragility, often raised in debates about #ALM.[13] Working through this lens, we then discuss the ways our #ALM participants understood the countermovement. While our participants articulated many of the contours of traditional understandings of countermovements, they differed from traditional discussions of countermovement history in the way they articulated the status quo. Rather than reinvesting in the direction of the status quo, #ALM participants understood their countermovement as working toward social change, but, in their opinions, in a more constructive manner than BLM. The distinction #ALM participants drew was marked by concerns about segregation and conflict between citizens, so that, while displays of white fragility were not absent from their discussions of #ALM, they more often sought protection for others they understood as incapable of discussing race, rather than themselves.

Our intention is not to excuse or condone instances of #ALM rhetoric that damaged BLM's anti-racist work, which we both support. Rather, we hope to provide nuanced insights into #ALM users' understanding of and motivations for using the hashtag. Intention does not override impact. Still, we believe an analysis of intention and motivation can help separate moments that invite persuasion from those that foreclose it. Understanding that some #ALM posters were using the hashtag with racist, malicious intentions, we hope to humanize those who subscribe to the "generally decent, if misguided, belief that our society [is] a level playing field," in hopes of developing modes of persuasion that might reverse the harmful impacts of the counter-movement.[14]

WHITENESS AND COUNTERMOVEMENTS

Countermovements of the type illustrated by #ALM are as traditional as social movements. Tahi L. Mottl defines a countermovement as "a conscious, collective, organized attempt to resist or reverse social change."[15] In this way, both social movements and countermovements attempt to influence public policy, but in oppositional directions. As such, Lisa M. Gring-Pemble highlights, though countermovements and social movements are working opposite one another, they can both be understood as counterpublics.[16] As oppositional counterpublics, both social movements and countermovements flourish based on the context created by public discourse.[17] Despite the structural similarities, Robert Asen reminds us, countermovements have received much less scholarly attention than the social movements they oppose;[18] Jennifer Rose Mercieca rightly points out that "no one wants to be accused of making a hero out of antebellum slaveholders," or other backlash groups, for that matter.[19] Still, understanding that members of these groups feel the same emotional investment in the backlash movement that progressive leaders feel in liberation movements is key to fully understanding the mechanics of oppression and justice. In this section, we outline the ways countermovements and whiteness can be understood both separately and together.

Whereas the goals of BLM were based in anti-racist policy and stated on the Vision for Black Lives platform, the #ALM countermovement was much less clear, blurring the lines of demarcation surrounding social movement studies. Robert S. Cathcart argues that the essence of a social movement lies in its rhetorical form.[20] The direction of this rhetorical form is important for differentiating social movements from countermovements.[21] On one hand, social movements attempt to persuade people outside the group, particularly agents of political change. This audience-centered imperative dictates the style and content of movement messaging. For many countermovements, on the other hand, the purpose of communication is not external persuasion, but rather internal solidarity. For example, Maddux explains, while suffragettes were focused on policy and governmental changes, anti-suffragettes shifted their focus to solidarity amongst themselves, often circulating communication only to other members of their established group rather than to readers outside its boundaries.[22] The standards of decorum are therefore set differently for countermovements and their internally focused communication than for social movements who must persuade outsiders.

Public discourses in general have been influenced by what Lauren Berlant describes as the turn to the intimate sphere, in which private, emotional experiences are politicized. In this context, publics and counterpublics often form around the affective and emotional experience of shared intimacy.[23] As Berlant writes, the contemporary political moment creates "a space of attachment and identification that is not saturated merely by ideological or cognitive content but is also an important sustainer of people's desires for reciprocity with the world."[24] In other words, the power of ideologically saturated discourse is only part of the sway of contemporary countermovements, as this type of rhetoric also works alongside the affective feelings of an emotional community. Emotions work within structures of privilege and oppression.[25] As such, groups that are both affective and focused on internal discourses can become echo chambers, circulating and recirculating messages that amplify both emotions and oppressive or resistant ideologies.

This simultaneously affective and ideological charge has been particularly salient in discussions of U.S. identity politics. For Maddux, countermovements, which overlap significantly with counterpublics, often spiral into internal discourses packed with fear appeals, including "conspiracy theories and apocalyptic warnings."[26] When a group's rhetoric reaches this point of irrationality, Steve Goodman writes, a deeply felt resistance builds against engaging outside discourses.[27] Even material evidence that could challenge the group's internally circulated worldview becomes fiercely threatening, and countermovements often respond reflexively and irrationally. At the same time, Allison B. Wolf writes, countermovement groups often frame their irrational and affectively based rhetorics as the only rational viewpoint in the conversation.[28] In doing so, these groups protect their own right to publicly express feelings while blocking the opposition's ability to do the same. Emotional appeals therefore self-perpetuate by justifying themselves as rational, while marking all other discourses as unreasonable.

Though these affective ideologies are rooted in internal discourse, they are importantly lived out through everyday interaction. That is, not only are these countermovements defined by the "social, political, and historical 'realities' produced by the rhetorical form,"[29] but as Bernadette Marie Calafell and Dawn Marie MacIntosh remind us, counterpublics are significantly defined by the "articulations of the everyday."[30] It is the material expression of affective ideologies that are of concern when we discuss privilege and oppression, and these play out not only through large-scale policy enactments but also through everyday exchanges. The intimacy in Berlant's intimate publics speaks not only to the affective dimension of the contemporary political moment, but also to the ways individual exchanges and performances reinforce messages and feelings from media, cultural forms, and political movements.[31]

WHITE FRAGILITY

Affective countermovement messaging and everyday lived experience both contribute to the maintenance of white supremacy in U.S. culture. White supremacy often manifests through a resistance to discussions of race, an intensely affective and reflexive performance by many Americans that bell hooks calls "a deep emotional investment in the myth of 'sameness.'"[32] This investment reflects the instability of whiteness as a naturalized ideological norm, particularly in an increasingly racially diverse country. As Ryan M. Crowley notes, because most white people never or very rarely confront the question of their race, many white people interpret their daily lives as unremarkable, despite the "litany of everyday advantages" afforded them by racial privilege.[33] Through this repetitive process, white privilege is naturalized so that, for white people, the most comfortable state of being is a continuation of the status quo.

Maintaining the status quo, by extension, often works through an insistence on white comfort, specifically the luxury of avoiding conversations about race and racism. As Robin DiAngelo writes, many white people experience and communicate extreme discomfort with approaching their own racial positionality.[34] DiAngelo describes this discomfort as "white fragility":

> White Fragility is a state in which even a minimum amount of racial stress becomes intolerable, triggering a range of defensive moves. These moves include the outward display of emotions such as anger, fear, and guilt, and behaviors such as argumentation, silence, and leaving the stress-inducing situation.[35]

The highly emotive and affective dimension of white fragility mirrors the conditions for countermovement formation we discussed earlier, and indeed white fragility works in much the same self-reinforcing way countermovement rhetoric often unfolds. Chris Linder identifies the "vivid descriptions of the fear associated with acting to address one's privilege";[36] these descriptions of racial conversations as threatening in turn work to shut down any possibility of discussing, let alone dismantling, white supremacy. Furthermore, Crowley points out, the de facto segregation that results from racist cultural politics is only exacerbated by this fear, so that white fragility continues to enclave white people away from discussions and consciousness of racial privilege.[37]

As useful as the term can be when applied accurately, white fragility has become a floating signifier in contemporary online discussion. Following DiAngelo's original work and continuing work by Joseph E. Flynn and others, the term seems most accurately applied to instances of active resistance to discussions of race among white people.[38] This resistance can take the form of professed indifference toward discussions of racial justice, a state Tyrone A. Forman termed "racial apathy,"[39] or something more explicit, as when discussants actively reassert their own whiteness or individual experience as central to the conversation.[40] Often in DiAngelo's work, the resistance of white fragility is totalizing, as participants actively remove themselves from conversations or refuse to participate.[41] As Cheryl E. Matias argues, such actions are the manifestation of the deeply unhealthy situation in which white children are denied access to understanding their own racial locations, causing "lasting emotional scars" that result in lashing out when race is raised as a topic of conversation.[42]

The active resistance to racial discussions by many white people takes place within a context that professes to value multiculturalism while disavowing conversations about systemic racism. Conversations in mainstream media often profess an interest in increasing diversity, but these same channels simultaneously avoid conversations regarding "police brutality, voter suppression, un-/under-employment, housing segregation, the achievement gap, the school-to-prison pipeline, [and] mass incarceration."[43] Richard Orozco and Jesus Jaime Diaz attribute this misalignment to an often unconscious but deeply felt connection to a culture that elevates whiteness.[44] This situation may not directly result in rejecting racial conversations, but it often manifests in a compulsion to prove white people's innocence, both generally and in the specific case of the white speaker. This is the pathway through which many white people profess interest in racial equality while disavowing actual political moves to remedy institutional threats against people of color.

Though this type of active resistance is common among white people asked to discuss race, discomfort with discussing race also manifests in seemingly more innocuous forms, particularly among white people beginning to engage anti-racist ideas. DiAngelo's concept of white fragility centers the idea that white people are not expected to engage with discussions of race,[45] but as Uma M. Jayakumar and Annie S. Adamian point out, many people who do regularly engage with people of color can behave in ways indicative of white fragility, even when they have learned insights about structures of white supremacy and institutional racism.[46] Flynn offers "white fatigue" as an additional term to distinguish between good and bad faith exhibitions of white resistance to racial conversation: [47]

> I define White fatigue as a temporary state in which individuals that are understanding of the moral imperative of antiracism disengage from or assume they no longer need to continue learning about how racism and/or White privilege function due to a simplistic understanding of racism as primarily individual. [48]

This fatigue can also take the form of engagement with other types of intersectional analysis, in which participants turn to analyses of gender or class as a way to mitigate conversations. [49] While these tactics distract from racial conversations, Flynn explains that they can nonetheless be important steps in the process of shifting logics of race for white people. [50]

WHITENESS AND FRAGILITY IN CONTEXT

We raise the issue of white fragility alongside other concepts like racial apathy and white fatigue to better address what was, for us, a somewhat surprising finding among our participants. Though many of the responses in our data could be characterized by DiAngelo's concept, often these responses emerged from people of color as well as white people. [51] Such a finding challenges aspects of DiAngelo's conception of fragility, moving more in the direction of Flynn's work, since obviously Black Memphians do not live in the shelter of exclusively white interactions DiAngelo spends much of her germinal article describing. [52] However, we agree with DiAngelo's contention that these reactions are inspired by a culture that prioritizes whiteness and white supremacy. Missing from her argument and its deployment in online spaces is the pervasiveness of the culture of whiteness, and the ways this enforced domination is often internalized by people of color, either subconsciously or as a way of navigating a hostile cultural context. As we argue in this chapter, the concept of white fragility is obviously useful, given its widespread popularity, but the concept of resistance to racial discussion as a reinforcement of status quo racial subordination deserves more attention and refinement. In the next section, we detail the ways our participants both enacted and resisted white fragility in their discussions of the #ALM countermovement.

The emergence of #ALM in the weeks following BLM's momentum as a social movement, as well as co-opted use of the "Lives Matter" portion of the title, make #ALM a clear illustration of a countermovement. As Chafetz and Dworkin write, this type of countermovement, which they correctly term a "backlash," is most likely to emerge when the social movement it opposes grows powerful or effective enough to pose as a threat. [53] Indeed, at the time #ALM emerged, references to BLM had appeared in numerous national news

and entertainment publications, and a Memphis branch of the national movement had been established and publicized in the greater city area. BLM, like
most social movements, took on the characteristic form of "confrontational
rhetoric," pushing back against injustices in various systems tied to racial
inequality.[54] As Burt Useem and Mayer N. Zald write, the success of a social
movement like BLM breaks ground for the success of its own countermovement, demonstrating the process of organization, the visibility of demonstration, and the potential effectiveness of group coalition building.[55] Perhaps as
a result, #ALM members mimicked many of the same discursive strategies
they perceived in BLM.

Many participants described BLM as a violent organization, an argument
that both draws from historical stereotypes of Black women and men as
angry, aggressive, and dangerous and that reverses the heart of BLM's con-
frontations regarding the violence enacted on Black bodies and communities
by police. Describing a video and several posts she had seen on Facebook,
Athena (27, White, Self-Employed) described a rally calling for justice for
Trayvon Martin as "Blacks slashing out against whites. I mean, fighting. . . .
They get violent. Really, really violent." When pressed for more detail, she
continued, "Killings. They'll rape and kill and just go on. . . . I see a lot more
beatings and . . . it's just all down Facebook. Them talking about little bitty
babies that'll be lined up. You'll see them decapitated." Athena's example is
extreme, but often our participants felt that BLM promoted violence. Brenda
(67, White, Retired Business Owner) worried that police were "scared to stop
anybody, that they may be killed or have their picture taken, perceive that
they did something wrong," and Diamond (34, Black, Retirement Specialist)
similarly noted, "There is a problem. . . . I used to be a police dispatcher. The
police are scared of everybody." In these cases, police violence against Black
men and women, an original impetus for BLM's formation, is reversed so
that the true violence stems from BLM and not from state violence against
Black bodies. As the literature on countermovements would predict, these
comments are both emotionally charged and, as Athena's example demonstrates, more graphic than might be expected to circulate in the general public.

The violence attributed to BLM sometimes took forms other than overt
physical violence. Just as Brenda, in the above quote, elided physical violence with the discursive violence of having one's picture spread across
social media, many of our participants perceived BLM as perpetuating online
violence. Succinctly put by Erykah (36, Black/Native, Massage Therapist/
Artist), "the actual objective of Black Lives Matter is to be disturbance."
This disturbance was acutely felt by Steve (58, White, Locksmith), who
bemoaned his son's allegiance to BLM and social justice. Steve said, "If
someone in our family—my brother-in-law is famous for this—would say
something that might be overtly racial, racist, [my son] would pretty much

jump all over him, and they have got into all kinds of fights over stuff like that."

Steve's story positions his son as the attacker, rather than his brother-in-law who is making "overtly . . . racist" comments. Moreover, Steve frames this attack using language of physical violence. On hearing the racist comments, his son "jump[s] all over" the man. This rhetorical approach represents an enactment of white fragility. DiAngelo and Özlem Sensoy note that white people often use metaphors of physical violence to describe moments in which they were confronted with their own racist actions. In this way, white people "project racist ideologies onto racialized people, and in so doing, re-inscribe White supremacy."[56] In DiAngelo and Sensoy's work, white people usually use metaphors of physical violence to depict people of color harming them. In this case, Steve's son is white, but because he has "swallowed [BLM's messages] hook, line, and sinker," he embodies the threat of violence otherwise attributed to people of color.

This tactic of rhetorically reversing patterns of violence to frame white people as victims of BLM's messaging was common among our #ALM respondents. As in the case of Steve and his family, though, this enactment of fragility was dictated more by affiliation within BLM or #ALM than it was by race of the speakers. For example, Tasha (37, Black, Teacher) worried that BLM encouraged division and violence both in the city and at a national level, describing the messaging surrounding BLM as a "vigilante type attitude." Such language reverses the demonstrated case of Trayvon Martin's murder at the hands of actual vigilante George Zimmerman. BLM's role of responding to vigilante violence is reframed as vigilante violence itself. Notably, Tasha is a Black woman, a demographic common among our #ALM participants. Additionally, though, her concern is not with being corrected about racist and white-centered viewpoints, as is common in DiAngelo and Sensoy's research. Rather, at issue is not race, but the messaging tactics used by a racial justice organization. The pivot on which the figurative language of violence is reversed is not in terms of race, but in terms of movement politics. In addition to vigilante violence, this also emerged in relation to police. Shelby (52, White, Physical Therapist) argued that "police officers are convicted by Black Lives Matter before they've even had a chance." Rather than using language of physical violence, as DiAngelo and Sensory predict, Shelby chooses the term "convict" to argue that police officers should have an opportunity for a trial and presumption of innocence, which is not afforded to people killed by police. Though Shelby may have demonstrated white fragility if confronted about her racial ideas, central to our analysis here is that the patterns of fragility projected onto the messaging tactics of an organization rather than discussions of race itself.

The turn in this discursive form of violence attribution lies in the ways literal, physical violence is weighed against the discursive violence of online

messaging or in-person conversation. In these cases, #ALM affiliates engaged BLM as a necessarily violent organization, which allowed them to
mobilize themselves and others in a countermovement against BLM. Though
sometimes participants provided examples of actual violence, as in Athena's
example of decapitated babies, more often the violence was simply sensed, as
when messages themselves felt like violent attacks. In this way, #ALM participants borrowed BLM's focus on violence. This rhetorical strategy was
more effective than dismissing or even countering BLM's anti-violence message because it allowed #ALM affiliates to claim the moral stance of affirming life while reaping the affective intensity of violent imagery and messaging. This move, of deploying emotion to flip the script on BLM's discussion
of actual state-sponsored violence, occurred throughout our interviews, demonstrating the ways countermovements are nourished by the co-optation of
social movement rhetoric.

PROJECTING SEGREGATION

A glaring example of this type of rhetorical turn lies in the ways #ALM-
affiliated participants flipped the issue of segregation, central to civil rights
struggles both in the 1960s and contemporary Memphis, positioning BLM
organizers and participants as the aggressors and themselves as victims. Mirroring the widely recognized historical laws that segregated schools, bath-
rooms, water fountains, and other public spaces, the less recognized de facto
patterns in Memphis mark the city as the fourth most segregated city in
America.[57] Just as in the twentieth century, this segregation has dramatically
impacted opportunities for education, housing, government contracts, and
other economic areas in the city of Memphis, and these points have all been
raised by protesters affiliated with BLM Memphis.[58] Though issues caused
directly by historical and contemporary segregation are at the heart of BLM's
mission, the #ALM participants we interviewed often attributed contemporary segregation not to white supremacist systems but to the rhetoric of BLM.

In labeling BLM a pro-segregation group, our participants often referenced the harmful historical and contemporary effects of racial separation
and subjugation as a way to advocate for #ALM. Many participants used
history to justify their choice to support #ALM over BLM. Directly referencing historical segregation, Beth (57, Black, Retired) told us "if you stop at
Black Life Matters, I'm sorry, but you're just segregating yourselves. If you
add the 'too,' it doesn't put the push on what Dr. King spoke against, desegregation." This strategy allowed #ALM supporters to demonstrate their
thoughtfulness, implying that BLM's messaging was neither insightful nor
sound. Pat (57, White, Marketing Director) indicated choosing #ALM for
this reason when she noted, "I immediately thought, you know, how divisive

is Black Lives Matter? . . . When I started looking at some of the leaders, they're very young kids . . . they don't really have a good grasp of history." Ashley (26, Black, Waitress), too, mentioned being drawn in to #ALM through references to history, particularly those that referenced the histories of groups like "Jews, Irish, Spanish, all kinds of people were oppressed." Particularly for those who would not typically be expected to affiliate with #ALM over BLM, including the two Black women quoted here, offering a historical analysis of sorts allowed them to demonstrate the thought they had put into their affiliation choice. Rather than adopt and understand BLM's interpretation of history, they used historical oppression and segregation as a way of defending #ALM.

While some participants saw BLM as exercising the same types of historical, de jure segregation at issue in the 1960s civil rights movement, others saw the contemporary movement as separating people by focusing on Black lives specifically. Derek (31, Black, Teacher) echoed Beth's focus on separating from other races, but he was particularly concerned about feelings of division and conflict in contemporary American culture. For Derek, BLM's focus on Black lives meant "you're not saying, white lives matter, Asian lives matter, Mexican lives matter, you're just saying Black lives matter. . . . All Lives Matter is . . . it's not anything to do with races. Everybody come together. It's trying to fix this broken reparation, division right now." The sense that contemporary politics was overly combative, and that this sense of conflict prevented progress in city and national issues, is reflected here. Such a perspective neglects to mention the political toll of anti-Black racism itself. Raising the issue of racism, for these participants, is akin to adding a new item to the agenda, rather than calling attention to something that has undergirded the entire American political system. Participants like Derek and Shelby, then, struggled to see BLM's focus on anti-Black politics as a route to addressing issues in the city and country. Instead, as Shelby noted, she and her friends "couldn't support, you know, a movement that, you know, wasn't about all lives but was separating and not really focusing on the issues that we thought were so detrimental." These detrimental issues, she added, included a crumbling public school system and increasing poverty in the city, issues at the core of BLM Memphis that are inarguably linked to the history of racial violence, discrimination, and, perhaps ironically, de jure and de facto segregation. These references to separation, when placed in the context of the ways racially divided cities like Memphis have nourished inequality, demonstrate a turning of the anti-segregation argument taken up by 1960s civil rights leaders. By attributing segregation to BLM, these participants turned the focus of the conversation away from the issues they referenced and back toward the group trying to address them.

The justification for choosing #ALM over BLM focused not only on the idea that BLM was segregationist, but also on the idea that #ALM offered the necessary unifying force for the city and country in general. Framing #ALM and desegregation as an obvious investment, Athena told us that, for her, #ALM means "that it should be unsegregated. Everybody has the right to live. Everybody has the right to equal rights on anything. To vote, to give their opinion. It should be unsegregated. Point-blank." Advocating for these equal rights, to Athena and others, should be done as a universal cause, rather than by identifying areas in which some identity groups face discrimination. Robert (21, Black, Material Handler) supported this idea, noting that "all is one works better than separating. You can stop one group of people. When it's a lot of groups of people, [that] works better. [When] all the groups of people were together and work together." Shelby similarly noted that "we need to just stop looking at ways to separate us and maybe find ways to bring us together." The idea that #ALM could work as a unifying force for positive change was perhaps the most common sentiment among our participants, most of whom felt that the discursive separation of races marked by BLM was more problematic than the actual de facto separation of racial communities within the city and country as a whole. Here again, this feeling is just that: a feeling. For white participants, the driving force seems to be the immediacy of feeling oneself excluded from a group, while Black #ALM participants expressed concern about excluding others. Rather than taking up history as a way to understand the contemporary legacy of anti-Black racism, participants saw de jure segregation and overt discrimination as a relic of the distant past. This attribution therefore turned civil rights arguments against BLM's advocacy.

Christine Sleeter describes the impetus for white people to reinforce a sense of racial solidarity with one another as "white racial boding."[59] In this case, though, many Black participants supported the idea of unity as well, even in the face of evidence that Memphis was not currently affording them, and those who looked like them, the same rights as their white counterparts. Rather than demonstrating DiAngelo's concept of white fragility, then, the racially unified fragility of our #ALM participants was much more firmly rooted in general challenges to the status quo. Understandings of historical and contemporary injustice that did not center anti-Black racism provided leverage for #ALM, as the countermovement offered a stabilizing commitment to the status quo.

IN DEFENSE OF THE STATUS QUO

A primary vehicle for the project of #ALM's discursive anti-segregation is the assumption that the status quo in the city and country is one of unity. The idea that BLM is responsible for dividing people is only salient in a context that assumes a pre-existing state of unity and equality. DiAngelo and Sensoy identify this as an aspect of white fragility, noting a reluctance to acknowledge systems of power, as though discussing inequality would conjure it into being.[60] Though participants in their study listened to repeated stories from people of color about the ways inequality and disunity manifested in their lives, white participants seemed unable to accept these stories. As they note, for many white people, accepting the stories of people of color feels "'dangerous' as it violates the imagined story of an America in which 'we are all united.'"[61] This type of behavior aligns these participants with Chafetz and Dworkin's concept of vested interest groups, as these groups "come to perceive one or more of [a social movement's] demands as antithetical to their interests," and as a result develop a vehement resistance to the movement's ideas.[62] Importantly, though, as Maddux writes, counterpublic groups, like those who band together to support status quo social structures in the face of BLM's messaging,[63] come from a variety of social locations and are not as easily identifiable as DiAngelo and Sensoy's analysis might indicate.[64] Whether or not they are united by race, these groups are always united by their ideological commitments.

To maintain the argument that unity and equality are status quo, many of our #ALM affiliates emphasized agreement by people of color. Brenda, for example, cited two Black Memphians, Reverend DeAndre Brown, a pastor who founded a nonprofit to support people when they are released from prison, and Fred Davis, who participated in the sanitation workers' strike and opened the city's first Black-owned insurance company. Brenda insistently told us about points of agreement between her position as an #ALM supporter and these two prominent Black men. For example, to emphasize her agreement with Davis's billboards about violence within Memphis's poor Black communities, she told us that what Davis "has come up with is, is the real issue" and that "he's hit the nail on the head." Though the oft-cited concept of "Black-on-Black crime" emerged frequently with our participants, the context of this issue was sometimes surprising; many of our participants raised this talking point outside conversations about violence, instead using the point to emphasize agreement between themselves and people of color in the city and country. Brenda's comment about the billboards followed from her point about Fred Davis, not from a conversation about violence. Similarly, though as a Black man, Derek may not have needed to appeal to Black agreement, he cited Martin Luther King Jr. in this way. He told us, "Black Lives Matter, it's just like one race, and that's not what Martin Luther King died for. He died for equality between races." Several of our participants cited King in this way, indicating that the civil rights leader would have been more supportive of #ALM than BLM. By emphasizing their agreement with Black leaders, these participants attempted to demonstrate that #ALM's positions were not racist or oppositional to racial justice, since, as their arguments went, they were advocated by Black men.

Not only did our participants offer evidence that Black leaders supported their #ALM positions, but they also indicated that the problems in the status quo were not a result of racism, but of a lack of self-love in Black communities. Bob (50, White, Salesperson), for example, suggested that #ALM offered a way of urging people to believe in the value of their own lives. He suggested spreading the message of "All Lives Matter. You've got to tell that person that's . . . on the corner in [the predominantly Black neighborhoods of] Frayser or in South Memphis: 'You know what? Your life matters.'" Steve, similarly, complained that "Blacks themselves do not seem to value their own lives. Uh, I mean, all you have to do is log onto WORG.com [the local news site] and you get all the latest shootings and what have you." In these appeals, Bob and Steve shift the responsibility for addressing problems in the status quo. Attributing injustice to racism would necessitate change on their part, whereas blaming Black Memphians for a lack of self-love places responsibility on others.

As common as this perspective was among our white participants, though, it was also frequently shared by Black participants. Connecting issues of incarceration among Memphis's poor Black youth to problems with parenting, Tasha explained, "When your mama and your daddy curse you out or don't want to be with you. . . . Then [children] can't even see all lives matter cause their lives didn't matter to the person who's supposed to care about them." Like Bob and Steve, Tasha seemed genuinely sad for the children she described, sharing that she had seen some abuse and neglect among her students. For Tasha, though, #ALM's message was more salient than BLM, as it allowed her a sense of power and hope; if youth commit crimes because they do not feel loved, then Tasha's role as a teacher allowed her to make an impact. As understandably comforting as this perspective might be, the rhetorical effect of her positioning places responsibility on individuals rather than systems. Ashley, too, shifted the blame for problems of poverty and violence caused by systemic and institutional inequality onto a lack of Black self-care:

> Black people, like, it's another plot where you're just playing this race card and we should go ahead and get off of this now. Like, you've been milking this for years. It's been generations and generations of destroying your life, not passing down the proper tools and guidance that the younger generation needs, so they're destroying their lives and then you don't want to face yourself in the mirror and say, "Okay. Well, I pissed off my whole life and I didn't teach my kids anything and they didn't teach their kids anything and now we're, like, four generations into bums and I don't want to say it's because of me, so I'm gonna say it's because of the system. I'm gonna say it's because of the Man. I'm gonna say it's because of the white government and the Republicans keeping us down." That's what I think that is, more or less. I'm sorry. (laughs)

Through these beliefs that place the impetus for change within an apparently flawed Black self-esteem, #ALM advocates revealed a belief that the status quo might be sufficient, if only they could advocate effectively for Black self-love. This effectively shifts the burden of responsibility onto poor Black communities and releases from responsibility the systems of white supremacy that structure much of the city's resources. This deeply neoliberal position reveals these participants' unwillingness to question the current state of affairs within their city, while also allowing them to apparently advocate for positivity and care for others.

Defending the status quo, for our #ALM participants, meant both providing support from Black leaders and shifting blame away from systemic issues and onto individual problems. In this way, participants professed and often seemed deeply committed to the possibility of unity; for those who supported #ALM, this goal could only be achieved through the eradication of BLM, since they understood BLM as a divisive group. As Derek told us, the messaging of #ALM was in favor of unity, and his most salient contact involved the idea that "we all can work together and like make America back whole again." The idea that America was once whole, but is now divided, demonstrates the ideological approach of many within the #ALM community, as well as the emotional investment in positivity and hope at the expense of actual change.

WHITE FRAGILITY AND BEYOND

Either through projecting the cause of segregation onto a Black organization or through diverting attention from the issues raised by the organization, #ALM's defense of the status quo represents one common marker for white fragility. However, it is important to note that the contours of white fragility, as DiAngelo defines them, are both represented and complicated in our participants' accounts.[65] In this way, white fragility emerges in our data as an empty signifier in that nearly any response to racial conflict by a white person could be termed white fragility and attributed to an inability and resistance to engage with concepts of race. These responses in our data, though, were not marked by a resistance to consideration; in fact, many of our participants seemed to have spent a great deal of time reading, discussing, and formulating responses to particular queries. Neither were the markers of white fragility exclusive to white participants, instead being common across all of our participant list.

One of the primary explanations for affiliating with #ALM involved feelings that BLM was exclusionary. Ashley, for example, noted, "I can't really identify with the whole Black Lives Matter thing because we do matter, but everyone matters, so I think my personality more fits in with the group All

Lives Matter." Ashley is reticent to exclude those who do not look like her from a movement that she sees as centering the value of life. Similarly, Derek remarked that #ALM "means not, not just one lives matter, it, not one race, two lives matter, but everybody's lives matter." The idea that #ALM actually encompassed BLM was common among our participants, who often expressed the idea that #ALM could either work as a replacement for or a supplement to BLM. Bob, for example, believed that #ALM included Black lives, expressing a particular concern for the poor Black children his church centered in outreach. As he elaborated:

> All Lives Matter means that every single life, which is a precious gift from God, kay? Every life matters. Every single life. From the womb to the tomb. All life matters to God and it needs to matter to us. Every single life. Does it even mean life for that inner-city kid in Memphis? Absolutely.

The idea of valuing life often overshadowed participants' ability to understand BLM as a movement that would be inclusive. Tasha told us, "Black Lives Matter sometimes make you seem one sided. . . . I don't care what color you are, what religion, you know, I want everybody to be able to live a nice long life because . . . everybody is loved by somebody." In each of these cases, participants identified with #ALM because they felt that BLM was exclusive of others' experiences.

This explanation held true for participants who strongly centered police brutality as the impetus for the BLM movement. Brenda, Pat, Julio (26, Black, Real Estate Agent), and others discussed problems of police brutality as also impacting Latinx and white citizens as well, but Diamond and Erykah's remarks bear quoting at length. Our Black participants, including Diamond and Erykah, tended to offer more detailed explanations of how police brutality might impact non-Black citizens, perhaps indicating an analysis more connected to issues of state violence. Explaining what #ALM means to her, Diamond noted

> to me it means fair treatment of everyone, no matter what the circumstance. . . . No one should be facing prejudice . . . and everyone should be treated the same across the board, and no one's more important than the next person. . . . For instance, a lot, I know a lot about Black Lives Matter has to do with police brutality. One aspect of it, then, anyone that's brutalized by the police, not just African-Americans but anyone, no matter what their race, creed and color.

Here, Diamond acknowledges brutality against Black citizens like herself, but also expands this problem with a concern that others impacted by police violence are not represented by BLM. In her discussion, it was clear that

Diamond had particular connections that made her feel this way. The same was true of Erykah, who explained

> I follow a guy, um, he went out of town with his family. He was 32, and took synthetic marijuana, and he just kind of started hallucinating, so his parents pulled over and called the police. And the white gentleman was killed by the white officers, 'cause they tased him 15 times in a row, within a very short period of time. And so he ended up passing, and that was the All Lives Matter. His parents are [saying] . . . "My son matters too."

In both of these explanations, participants do not view BLM's focus on police brutality as being dismissed or watered down by their use of #ALM. Instead, they see the use of the countermovement hashtag as a way of bringing fairness and understanding to those outside their race, while acknowledging the problem of police violence.

In fact, this idea of acknowledging outside or additional problems in the world and believing those additional issues as being beyond the scope of BLM was very common. Geneva Gay and Kipchonge N. Kirkland describe the common tactic within white fragility in which speakers conjure issues of gender or class as a way of avoiding conversations about race.[66] This tactic, Flynn believes, should not always be viewed as an expression of resistance to racial discussions; rather, it can in some circumstances indicate a moment of fatigue in learning about social inequality.[67] While we cannot vouch for the commitment of our participants to learning about social issues based on a single interview, many of our participants did raise issues that should be addressed in an intersectional frame. Max (19, Black, Receptionist) affiliated with #ALM because "every cause falls under All Lives Matter: Black Lives Matter, equal wages matter, you know, women should get paid same as men for the same job matter, immigration matter. You know, everything falls under the umbrella." Brenda similarly saw #ALM as addressing "all of the issues we have that need to be solved for the betterment of mankind." Erykah spoke specifically of advocating for LGBTQ rights, believing that, in that case, #ALM was more appropriate than BLM. Jesse (25, White, Self-Employed) brought up homelessness, Beth raised the issue of domestic violence, and Pat recounted growing up "in the rural south, which is still one of the four major poverty areas of the country. And I have relatives that live in trailers . . . some of them didn't even graduate from high school." Of course, these issues do not preclude BLM from use. Not only does BLM's founding by three queer women of color clearly center intersectionality, but as we discussed in the previous chapter, many of our BLM affiliates specifically noted intersectionality as an important aspect of their group membership. Still, it indicates a possibility that, for some participants, #ALM opened the possibility of considering intersectional forms of violence and oppression, rather than exclusively demonstrating an enactment of white fragility, as many popular press articles suggested. Undoubtedly some users of #ALM were not invested in social justice. Others, though, as those we have quoted here, seem more open to learning and expanding the reach of BLM, rather than exclusively countering the movement that they ostensibly agreed with on many issues.

To be clear, instances of white fragility were not absent from our interviews, and the interview situation, in which participants voluntarily came in to speak with us about the predetermined topic of #ALM, is not the same type of context in which DiAngelo explores issues of white fragility.[68] The primary area in which white fragility emerged, though, was not in displays by white participants, but rather in descriptions from Black participants. Allie (57, Black, Retired) summarized this perspective best when she observed, "[People] are saying, with All Lives Matter, 'I'm white. My life matters too. . . . I'm just as important as you.'" Erykah who, like Allie, supported both BLM and #ALM, agreed that BLM could be offensive to some, explaining that some people used #ALM "because they don't want to offend anyone, and they were scared to take a stand . . . so not to hurt anyone's feelings, all lives matter." Whereas Erykah felt #ALM was used to avoid offending others, Julio believed that #ALM was popular because non-Black users wanted to have their own problems acknowledged. He remarked, "I do think that folks use it to kind of say, 'Well, you know, there's bad things happening to you, but there's bad things happening to us as well. And our problems may not be as publicized as your problems, but, you know, don't forget about us, or don't forget our problems.'" In these examples, Black participants describe the perception that #ALM offers a more accessible way of explaining issues of inequality to non-Black friends. As Max further explained, BLM and #ALM, as movement and countermovement, positioned people as oppositional. For him, "a person might not, you know, quote/unquote, be racist, but they don't feel like you have to say Black lives matter [instead of] all lives matter." In other words, the two phrases were somewhat interchangeable and definitely combinable for Max, as with many of our Black participants.

Other Black participants expressed feeling hurt by members of their community and family who assumed that #ALM indicated a dissociation from their racial identity. Speaking succinctly, Derek noted, "We're not white racists and bitchin' and all that," a phrase that certainly would qualify as an expression of white fragility if spoken by a white person. Ashley angrily recounted several encounters with her sister that culminated in her asking her sibling not to return to her home. One of these, she explained as:

> [My sister will] come over to my house and . . . she can just be scrolling down Facebook and then, you know, I'll share something and then she'll see it and then she'll go to cackling about it, and I'm like, "You know, if that's not how

you feel, then that's your opinion. My opinion is mine." And then she'll go to talking about all kinds of other, you know, racist crap and I'm like, you know, "Now, I have to remove you. Now, I have no choice but to ask you to leave each and every time." To the point that she was, like, you know, "You're an Uncle Tom and blah, blah, blah, blah, and I don't even want to be around you" and I'm like, "That's fine. It's perfectly fine."

In this way, the concept of white fragility as an integral aspect of #ALM was felt as a harm to these participants. While they understood themselves as operating within a framework of openness, others in their community believed that all #ALM posters were speaking from a position of white supremacy. Instead, many of #ALM affiliates we interviewed felt drawn to expand the notion of equality in ways they felt BLM could not capture.

We highlight these complications to white fragility within our study not to refute the existence of resistance to racial conversations, which of course are prominent and increasing in extremity in our current cultural context. Instead, we want to broaden the ways this affectively rooted resistance is understood, such that it can emerge in a variety of complex and often unpredictable forms. Responses that could be coded as white fragility can actually represent a wide range of responses, including white fatigue,[69] racial apathy,[70] cognitive dissonance over the nature of the issue at hand, or a feeling of being overwhelmed by the many social issues circulated through social media.

CONCLUSION

Though we expected the responses to our #ALM interviews to be both primarily white in racial identification and primarily racist in ideological character, in fact the #ALM affiliates we spoke with represented a much more complex and nuanced approach to social issues than we had anticipated. Just as Zald and Useem's framework might have predicted, the same issues emerged in discussions of #ALM as of BLM, largely because BLM emerged first, initiated the conversation, and was considerably more organized and focused.[71] Yet, in this case at least, the demonstrations of resistance to BLM were not marked by the type of white fragility one might expect, given #ALM's orientation against a movement designed to end violence against African Americans. The #ALM participants we interviewed instead demonstrated a somewhat scattered relationship to BLM in that posters were not united, nor did they agree on the value or purpose of the countermovement. #ALM Memphis therefore offered a challenge to the ways scholars and the public tend to think about both countermovements and Black/white racial dynamics. Instead, their responses point to the fact that history is rarely written in black and white. Rather, the complex organizing and counterorganizing that has marked Memphis's racial politics often found allies in unlikely places and from unlikely races.

This chapter has underscored the general meanings of #ALM for its affiliates through a lens of countermovement rhetoric and white fragility. As a countermovement, #ALM demonstrates the importance of history, interpreted through a lens of personal experience, to recruiting countermovement affiliates. Much of BLM's strength flows from the ability of affiliates to share videos, images, and other messaging formats, particularly those documenting police violence and other instances of racial injustice through social media. Referencing Berlant's work,[72] Joshua Gunn describes an intimate public as "a people brought into being through the consumerist circulation of personal or private experiences."[73] While this concept is rooted in Berlant's analysis of commercially circulated content,[74] Gunn's description highlights the importance of personal connection to content. The individual histories participants brought to social media and offline conversations shaped the ways they understood BLM and #ALM as speaking to histories of violence. When a message spoke particularly to their understanding of personal and cultural history, they understood the associated movement or hashtag as speaking to them as well. The affiliation of sometimes unlikely members with #ALM and BLM, then, can only be understood within the context of the emotive publics created by the multi-format nature of social media. For #ALM members in particular, affiliation was often more strongly driven by feeling than reason.

As with the account that began this chapter, the seemingly infinite strands of thought that circulate through Facebook, Twitter, Instagram, Medium, and other messaging platforms are unpredictable and varied. This means that, while many white social media users certainly used #ALM as a way of silencing BLM, many other social media users saw the hashtag in a different light.[75] Indeed, one of the most surprising findings for us was the way that many of our participants saw the two hashtags not as oppositional, but as complementary, with many of our Black participants including both hashtags in many of their posts. We understand this complication as indicative of dichotomization that marks many historical discussions of race and social movements. Framings of the civil rights movement in educational and media contexts often downplay the historical role of white allies and Black opposition to mid-twentieth-century organizing. This legacy continues to emerge in traditional and social media, shaping many cultural conversations that paint Black and white as monolithic. Humans are messy, and as such, so are the racial identifications and disidentifications those humans express. Social media may complicate this situation, but perhaps it only makes visible the complications that have been present all along.

NOTES

1. Diamond Alexis, "Chilli Responds to 'All Lives Matter' Backlash," *BET*, May 2017, http://www.bet.com/music/2017/05/10/tlc-chilli-all-lives-matter.html.

2. Jesse Damiani, "Every Time You Say 'All Lives Matter' You Are Being an Accidental Racist," *Huffington Post*, July 15, 2016, http://www.huffingtonpost.com/jesse-damiani/every-time-you-say-all-li_1_b_11004780.html.

3. Madeleine Sweet, "'Separate but Equal,' #AllLivesMatter and Rewording the Reign of White Supremacy," *Huffington Post*, August 10, 2016, http://www.huffingtonpost.com/entry/separate-but-equal-alllivesmatter-and-rewording_us_57ab8e5ce4b091a07ef86347.

4. Nikita Carney, "All Lives Matter, but So Does Race: Black Lives Matter and the Evolving Role of Social Media," *Humanity and Society* 40, no. 2 (2016).

5. The Movement for Black Lives, "Platform. A Vision for Black Lives," retrieved from https://policy.m4bl.org/platform/; BLMM, "About: #BlackLivesMatter Memphis Chapter," retrieved from https://Blacklivesmattermemphis.wordpress.com/about/.

6. Carney, "All Lives Matter."

7. Carimah Townes, "Obama Explains the Problem with 'All Lives Matter,'" *Think Progress,* last updated October 22, 2015, retrieved from https://thinkprogress.org/obama-explains-the-problem-with-all-lives-matter-780912d54888.

8. Eduardo Bonilla-Silva, *Racism without Racists: Color-Blind Racism and Racial Inequality in Contemporary America* (3rd ed.). (Lanham, MD: Rowman & Littlefield, 2010); Mark Orbe, "#AllLivesMatter as Post-Racial Rhetorical Strategy," *Journal of Contemporary Rhetoric* 5, no. 3/4 (2015).

9. Robin DiAngelo, "White Fragility," *International Journal of Critical Pedagogy* 3, no. 3 (2011): 54.

10. Janet Saltzman Chafetz and Anthony Gary Dworkin, "In the Face of Threat: Organized Antifeminism in Comparative Perspective," *Gender & Society* 1, no. 1 (1987).

11. Kristy Maddux, "When Patriots Protest: The Anti-Suffrage Discursive Transformation of 1917," *Rhetoric & Public Affairs* 7, no. 3 (2004).

12. David S. Meyer and Suzanne Staggenborg. "Movements, Countermovements, and the Structure of Political Opportunity," *American Journal of Sociology* 101, no. 6 (1996).

13. See for example Alissa Greenberg, "What the Woman Who Invented the Term 'White Fragility' Thinks about Trump," *The Stranger*, last updated April 5, 2017, retrieved from https://www.thestranger.com/features/2017/04/05/25056620/what-the-woman-who-invented-the-term-white-fragility-thinks-about-trump; Sincere Kirabo, "Why White America Demonizes the #BlackLivesMatter Movement—And Why That Must Change," *The Establishment*, last updated February 18, 2017, retrieved from https://theestablishment.co/why-white-america-demonizes-the-Blacklivesmatter-movement-and-why-that-must-change-4cda83727063.

14. Catherine Squires, Eric King Watts, Mary Douglas Vavrus, Kent A. Ono, Kathleen Feyh, Bernadette Marie Calafell, and Daniel C. Brouwer, "What Is This 'Post-' in Postracial, Postfeminist . . . (Fill in the Blank?)," *Journal of Communication Inquiry* 34, no. 3 (2010): 222.

15. Tahi L. Mottl, "An Analysis of Countermovements," *Social Problems* 27, no. 5 (1980): 620.

16. Lisa M. Gring-Pemble, "'It's We the People . . . , Not We the Illegals': Extreme Speech in Prince William County, Virginia's Immigration Debate," *Communication Quarterly* 60, no. 5 (2012).

17. Meyer and Staggenborg, "Movements, Countermovements."

18. Robert Asen, "Ideology, Materiality, and Counterpublicity: William E. Simon and the Rise of a Conservative Counterintelligentsia," *Quarterly Journal of Speech* 95, no. 3 (2009).

19. Jennifer Rose Mercieca, "The Culture of Honor: How Slaveholders Responded to the Abolitionist Mail Crisis of 1835," *Rhetoric & Public Affairs* 10, no. 1 (2007): 53.

20. Robert S. Cathcart, "A Confrontation Perspective on the Study of Social Movements," *Central States Speech Journal* 34, no. 1 (1983).

21. Maddux, "When Patriots Protest."

22. Ibid.

23. Lauren Berlant, *The Female Complaint: The Unfinished Business of Sentimentality in American Culture* (Durham, NC: Duke University Press, 2008).

24. Ibid., x–xi.

25. Cheryl E. Matias, "'And Our Feelings Just Don't Feel It Anymore': Re-Feeling Whiteness, Resistance, and Emotionality," *Understanding & Dismantling Privilege* 4, no. 2 (2014).

26. Maddux, "When Patriots Protest," 303.

27. Steve Goodman, *Sonic Warfare: Sound, Affect, and the Ecology of Fear* (Cambridge, MA: The MIT Press, 2010).

28. Allison B. Wolf, "'Tell Me How That Makes You Feel': Philosophy's Reason/Emotion Divide and Epistemic Pushback in Philosophy Classrooms," *Hypatia* 32, no. 4 (2017).

29. Cathcart, "A Confrontation Perspective," 70.

30. Bernadette Marie Calafell and Dawn Marie MacIntosh, "Latina/o Vernacular Discourse: Theorizing Performative Dimensions of an Other Counterpublic," in *What Democracy Looks Like: The Rhetoric of Social Movements and Counterpublics*, edited by Christina R. Foust, Amy Pason, and Kate Rogness Zittlow (Tuscaloosa: University of Alabama Press, 2017), 38.

31. Berlant, *The Female Complaint*.

32. bell hooks, *Black Looks: Race and Representation* (New York: South End Press, 1992), 167.

33. Ryan M. Crowley, "Transgressive and Negotiated White Racial Knowledge," *International Journal of Qualitative Studies in Education* 29, no. 8 (2016): 1017.

34. DiAngelo, "White Fragility."

35. Ibid., 54.

36. Chris Linder, "Navigating Guilt, Shame, and Fear of Appearing Racist: A Conceptual Model of Antiracist White Feminist Identity Development," *Journal of College Student Development* 56, no. 6 (2015): 549.

37. Ibid.

38. DiAngelo, "White Fragility"; Joseph E. Flynn, Jr., "White Fatigue: Naming the Challenge in Moving from an Individual to a Systemic Understanding of Racism," *Multicultural Perspectives* 17, no. 3 (2015): 115–24.

39. Tyrone A. Forman, "Color-Blind Racism and Racial Indifference: The Role of Racial Apathy in Facilitating Enduring Inequalities," in *The Changing Terrain of Race and Ethnicity*, eds. Maria Krysan and Amanda E. Lewis (New York: Russel Sage Foundation, 2004).

40. Cheryl E. Matias, "'Why Do You Make Me Hate Myself?'": Re-Teaching Whiteness, Abuse, and Love in Urban Teacher Education," *Teaching Education* 27, no. 2 (2016).

41. DiAngelo, "White Fragility."

42. Matias, "'Why Do You Make Me Hate Myself?'" 194.

43. Flynn, "White Fatigue," 119.

44. Richard Orozco and Jesus Jaime Diaz, "'Suited to Their Needs': White Innocence as a Vestige of Segregation," *Multicultural Perspectives* 18, no. 3 (2016).

45. Diangelo, "White Fragility."

46. Uma M. Jayakumar and Annie S. Adamian, "The Fifth Frame of Colorblind Ideology: Maintaining the Comforts of Colorblindness in the Context of White Fragility," *Sociological Perspectives* 60, no. 5 (2017).

47. Flynn, "White Fatigue," 115.

48. Ibid., 117

49. Crowley, "Transgressive and Renegotiate."

50. Flynn, "Color-Blind Racism."

51. DiAngelo, "White Fragility."

52. Ibid.; Flynn, "Color-Blind Racisim."

53. Chafetz and Dworkin, "In the Face of Threat."

54. Cathcart, "A Confrontation Perspective," 70.

55. Burt Useem and Mayer N. Zald, "From Pressure Group to Social Movement: Organizational Dilemmas of the Effort to Promote Nuclear Power," *Social Problems* 30, no. 2 (1982).

56. Robin DiAngelo and Özlem Sensoy, "Getting Slammed: White Depictions of Race Discussions as Arenas of Violence," *Race Ethnicity and Education* 17, no. 1 (2014): 107.

57. Michael B. Sauter, Evan Comen, and Samuel Stebbins, "16 Most Segregated Cities in America," *24/7 Wall Street*, July 21, 2017, https://247wallst.com/special-report/2017/07/21/16-most-segregated-cities-in-america/.

58. BLMM, "About: #BlackLivesMatter Memphis Chapter." Retrieved from https://Blacklivesmattermemphis.wordpress.com/about/.

59. Christine Sleeter, "White Silence, White Solidarity," in *Race Traitor*, ed. Noel Ignatiev and John Garvey (New York: Routledge, 1996), 261.

60. DiAngelo and Sensoy, "Getting Slammed."

61. Ibid., 125.

62. Chefetz and Dworkin, "In the Face of Threats," 35.

63. Maddux, "When Patriots Protest."

64. DiAngelo and Sensoy, "Getting Slammed."

65. DiAngelo, "White Fragility."

66. Geneva Gay and Kipchonge N. Kirkland. "Developing Cultural Critical Consciousness and Self-Reflection in Preservice Teacher Education," *Theory into Practice* 42, no. 3 (2003).

67. Flynn, "White Fatigue."

68. DiAngelo, "White Fragility."

69. Flynn, "White Fatigue."

70. Forman, "Color-Blind Racism."

71. Useem and Zald, "From Pressure Groups."

72. Berlant, *The Female Complaint.*

73. Joshua Gunn, "On Speech and Public Release," *Rhetoric and Public Affairs* 13, no. 2 (2010): 180.

74. Berlant, *The Female Complaint.*

75. Robin L. Hughes and Natasha Flowers, "Colonizing Black Lives: The 'Crusade' for All Lives and White Fragility," *Diverse: Issues in Higher Education*, last updated January 31, 2016, retrieved from http://diverseeducation.com/article/80792/.

Chapter Three

The Spirit Led Me

Toward an Understanding of Religious
Rhetoric and Pentecostal Piety in the BLM Movement

In her important work chronicling the role of faith in the early days of the Ferguson resistance, Leah Gunning Francis argued that many of the BLM activists and protesters in the streets of Ferguson "demonstrated a very particular kind of embodiment of scripture and faith" and that activists "sought meaning through scripture in connection with their work for justice."[1] Gunning Francis offers an example of this in the testimony of Alexis Templeton. When speaking on the faith and spirituality of the protesters she met and marched with in the streets of Ferguson, Templeton noticed that protesters' spirituality seemed "fluid." She remarked, "When you're fluid in the Word, you live better because you're not constantly looking for the literal meaning in these scriptures. You are moving. You're just letting the Word push you. You're letting it come out of you. That's what you supposed to do."[2] It was the activists' responses and performances of faith that led Templeton to an epiphany in the streets of Ferguson. She confessed, "They taught me to believe in God, and that's real."[3]

Francis's book is important because it not only chronicles the early days of the Ferguson resistance and BLM's activism, but it also locates the role of faith in contemporary racial justice organizing. The relationship between religion and BLM has always been contentious. While BLM is often compared to the civil rights movement, in which the Black church and religious leaders like Martin Luther King, Jr. figured prominently, the contemporary movement is not often discussed as a spiritual or faith-inspired movement. The lack of attention to spirituality in BLM within mainstream public discourse highlights the perception that the Black church was silent during the early days of the movement. Senior pastor of Chicago's Progressive Baptist Church, Charlie Dates, illustrates the rift at work in this perceived silence. He laments that his "generation will have to give an account for our strange silence" regarding the BLM movement.[4] "This is the first time," he continued, "that the Black pulpit has not been at the forefront of the moral conversation of systemic injustice against Black people in America."[5] For many, the apparent lack of formal participation from Black churches around the country marked BLM as something different from the mid-twentieth-century civil rights movement, for better or for worse.

As church and movement leaders weighed in on the apparent rift between religion and justice in twenty-first-century organizing, differences in interpretation became clear. For Jamal Bryant, a protest leader both nationally and in his home city of Baltimore, the question is one of centrality. While church leaders had previously overlapped with movement leaders, BLM offers the challenge of reimagining racial justice organizing that decenters but still includes the role of faith. He asks, "How do you become a part of something that you don't lead?" answering his own query with a charge for churches to become more inclusive and reexamine theological positions on leadership and sexuality.[6] The need to explore oppressions like gender and sexuality that intersect with anti-Black racism became clear during the national call for a BLM Sunday on December 14, 2014. The call to pray for "Black males" in many churches was rebuffed by women and gay activists who demanded more inclusivity.[7]

Despite the apparent rift between the traditional role of the Black church in racial justice organizing and the contemporary BLM movement, the historical role of spirituality in Black liberation movements bubbles beneath the surface of BLM adherents' understandings of their activism. In this chapter, we focus on our participants' use of religious language and their own understandings of religion, faith, and spirituality that describe their involvement with BLM. While public discourses about religion within BLM frame faith as a contentious or unwelcomed issue, many BLM participants understand spirituality as central to the connection with the movement and Black liberation more generally. Though BLM arose as a secular movement, we argue that this does not mean that participants were "non-religious" or "anti-religious." Instead, for many participants, their positions within the church and the movement were mutually constitutive. By participating in BLM, they were driven to make their churches more inclusive, a point that was particularly challenging for white evangelical members of the movement. At the same time, though, participants of faith were often unable to separate their passion for the movement from their spiritual grounding, and many understood this as a continuation of the historical role of the Black church within the fight for racial justice. In short, religion functioned as a conduit between BLM and the histories of racial justice and oppression.[8]

BLM, PENTECOSTAL PIETY,
AND THE ROLE OF FAITH

Central to the conversation about the role of religion in BLM is a tension between church traditions and the changing faces of movement leadership and activism in general. This tension proves difficult to resolve, given the complex set of questions that have arisen from the church, non-religious BLM leaders and members, and faith-oriented BLM participants. While the conflict over religion in contemporary racial justice organizing often seems divisive, it also provides insights into the ways both the church and BLM offer feedback to one another, pushing religious organizations toward greater inclusivity while consistently highlighting the historical significance of the church in justice work. Agreement over the role of the church may be contentious, but the discourses surrounding the role of religion in Black liberation are central to understanding the position of BLM as a continuation of historical social justice organizing.

Much of the tension stems from perceptions of irreconcilable ideological difference between traditional religious perspectives and those of contemporary social justice organizers. Public theologian and religion blogger Lisa Robinson suggests that for some people of faith, the problem with BLM lies in its ideological origins. She argues that "foundations matter," and if the foundation is flawed, then so is the whole movement. For Robinson, the primary issue lies in BLM's embrace of "a Marxist oriented philosophy that actually works against a Christian paradigm."[9] The idea that Marxism, in the philosophical and academic sense, runs counter to both racial justice organizing and the anti-poverty work central to Robinson's platform is surprising, given the centrality of Marxism to historical analyses of capitalism and the political position of the working poor. Yet for Robinson, the centrality of Marxism to the BLM platform is a matter of ethical adherence to the Christian "kingdom paradigm." BLM's basis in a viewpoint that is not explicitly Christian means that, for those like Robinson, "there are good and valid reasons for Christians to reject BLM as a legitimate Christian response to racial healing."[10] Those who identify as Christian and who support the idea that BLM runs in ideological contradiction to Christian theology, then, cannot reconcile their own personal histories and investments with a contemporary vision of racial justice founded outside the traditions of the church.

Robinson was not alone in her condemnation of BLM. As the movement grew, in apparent absence from the explicitly religious participation many had come to expect from Black liberation organizing, many struggled to make sense of a new tradition of racial justice that did not center the Black church. This move, for Religious Studies professor Anthony Bradley, was misguided. BLM, he writes, does not represent the Christian gospel, and that's fine. It never intended to. It did not emerge from the church. It's a social movement that does not presuppose the Triune God at the outset. Therefore, Christians need not employ any number of creative hermeneutics to attempt to theologically justify it, make it consistent with Christianity, or explain their proximity to it.[11]

Bradley's analysis is a stronger condemnation of BLM as secular that, in part, explains the ideological tension between some Christian traditions and the contemporary intersectional viewpoint of social justice organizing. BLM co-founders Patrisse Khan-Cullors, Opal Tometi, and Alicia Garza are not products of the Black Church.[12] Further, as Christopher A. House reminds us, the "intersectionality of their Black, gendered bodies and, for two of them, their self-identification as queer women, challenge the patriarchal culture and heteronormative gender roles of Black Church–led movements, specifically the Civil Rights Movement."[13] The centrality of intersectionality, which poses challenges both for traditional church-based movements and social movements in general, explains some of the foundational differences between movements based in religion and movements based in the complexity of contemporary identity politics.

Following the traditions of movement studies and public discourse surrounding social justice in general, such explanations centralize movement leaders and platforms. In doing so, they risk painting the activists within the movement with a broad, monolithic brush. This raises questions of how, in interpreting BLM as devoid of any religious ideology or foundation, people of faith reconcile BLM and their own religious beliefs. For House, this explanation lies in semantic renegotiation, as "many BLM activists self-identify as 'spiritual but not religious' and their activism is animated by a deep spirituality that is personal, yet not connected to a Black Church religious tradition or Afro-Protestantism."[14] One of the BLM founders, Patrice Khan-Cullors, seems to agree with House's assertion. In an interview with the online magazine *Religion Dispatches*, Khan-Cullors reports coming to this work from a "deep philosophical place that [asks], what does it take for humans to live in our full humanity and allow for others to live in their full dignity?"[15] Khan-Cullors does not believe that "spirit is this thing that lives outside of us dictating our lives, but rather our ability to be deeply connected to something that is bigger than us. I think that is what makes our work powerful."[16] This explanation more clearly reconciles spirituality with activism, explaining faith not as a barrier to activism, but as a bridge to understanding the role of justice beyond the individual experience. As she explains,

When you are working with people who have been directly impacted by state violence and heavy policing in our communities, it is really important that there is a connection to the spirit world. For me, seeking spirituality had a lot to do with trying to seek understanding about my conditions—how these conditions shape me in my everyday life and how do I understand them as part of a larger fight, a fight for my life. People's resilience, I think, is tied to their will to live, our will to survive, which is deeply spiritual. The fight to save your life is a spiritual fight.[17]

Flying in the face of explanations like Robinson's, then, Khan-Cullors's account of the role of spirituality in BLM is one of connection. Rather than preventing Christians from participating in BLM, the foundational philosophy of the movement is one of inclusivity and unity between the self and others.

The idea that spirituality allows for a deeper understanding of the self within a context of communal union offers a framing of BLM's philosophy that more closely aligns with some traditional readings of theology. Elise Edwards suggests that while people who are engaging through faith "know that social transformation involves politics and policy," they also believe that "transformative work is ultimately a spiritual effort that requires a shift in consciousness."[18] This type of transformation demands a reshaping of self that might also be described as "conversion."[19] While an interior reshaping of the self is not dependent upon membership or attachment to an organized religion, faith traditions can offer philosophical direction on how to imagine the connection of the self to a larger power. In fact, Edwards argues, the perspectives of traditional Black liberation organizations have historically drawn from Black theology for strategies of resistance and demands for justice and change.[20] From this perspective, not only have the Black church and liberation always been connected, but the entire contemporary viewpoint of racial justice organizing is inextricably linked to notions of faith and spirituality.

This analysis problematizes the separation of justice from theology present in many discussions of BLM. Rather than dividing faith from liberation, Andre Wilkes's notion of "Pentecostal Piety" aligns the two. Pentecostal piety

refers to the role of the Holy Spirit in political action. The Holy Spirit is a wellspring of solidarity that undergirds commitment to building a commonwealth, common good society among individuals of differing backgrounds and moral commitments. To riff on religion scholar Robert Bellah, Pentecostal piety is probably best thought of as a subversive civil religion. In its most radical variety, Pentecostal piety embodies a kind of democratic socialism.[21]

Despite the potential implications of the term, Wilkes's concept does not centralize any particular Christian denomination or any specific religious tradition. Instead, he offers the concept as one that crosses denominational, religious, faith, and moral lines based on the precedent of inter-faith justice work.

Although the civil rights movement is commonly linked with the Baptist denomination of Christianity, we don't do it justice to remember it as denominational simply because it was so strongly associated with a certain, charismatic
Christian clergyman of color. The ideas animating the movement were of far
more diverse origin. The civil rights movement saw Black folks (and non-
Black folks) consecrate the American dream by way of the prophetic Baptist
theology of Reverend Dr. Martin Luther King, yes. But it also involved the
anointed agnosticism of Southern Christian Leadership Conference's founding
executive director and the generative force of the Student Nonviolent Coordinating committee, Ella Baker. The radical Quaker vision of a Bayard Rustin
next to the ethical humanism of an Asa Phillip Randolph were also blended in.
And also in the mix was the subtle, yet significant tradition of faith-filled lay
activists like Fannie Lou Hamer and Marian Wright Edelman. [22]

As this account makes clear, the idea that the mid-twentieth-century civil
rights movement was decisively and singularly religious reflects a misremembering of the communal nature of 1960s Black liberation. Even among
leaders, the theology of the movement was unsettled, other than to recognize
the importance of working toward a cause larger than the individual.

Drawing from Wilkes, we note two major points about Pentecostal piety.
First, Pentecostal piety places a heavy emphasis on the role of the spirit.
Proponents of this type of spirituality are not locked into the rigid confines of
religious orthodoxy. In many cases, people practicing this brand of spirituality are not affiliated at all with any religious institution. They are free to
move as the spirit leads and guides. For example, as Johnson notes in his
autoethnography of the early movement, in Ferguson, many activists described feeling "called" or as though "something pulled me in that direction." [23] It was this talk of the spirit that led many people to join the Ferguson
resistance, and, consequently, many activists there interpreted their "call stories" as an extension of the spirit working in their lives. [24] In keeping with
Wilkes's notion of Pentecostal piety, that "something" led people to find
their own voices and discover their own gifts and talents. Moreover, it was
those voices, gifts, and talents that help lead to the establishment of building
a "common good society among individuals of differing backgrounds and
moral commitments." [25] While the spirit moved in those individuals, the spirit
also moved collectively and led many of those who joined to sense a new
community where they could set aside their differences and focus on what
brought them together.

Second, Pentecostal piety prioritizes prophetic action, framing particular
approaches to activism as a "subversive civil religion." [26] Prophetic, in this
context, refers to the crucial role of religion in offering a critical perspective
on justice, oppression, and the contours of a moral society in general. To
borrow Florian Horne's phrasing, prophetic witnessing "emphasize[s] the
critical role of religion rather than a comforting one." [27] Therefore, a person

or group who engages prophetic, or "critical," witness is pointing to the "distortions in society and criticizes injustice, exploitation, and oppression."[28] Framed in this way, BLM acts as a prophetic movement that provides witness to the contextual realities faced by many African Americans. In other words, BLM is part of the long African American prophetic tradition. Johnson writes of this tradition:

> Birth from slavery and shaped in Jim and Jane Crow America, the African American version of the prophetic tradition has been the primary vehicle that has comforted and given voice to many African Americans. Through struggle and sacrifice, this tradition has expressed Black people's call for unity and cooperation, as well as the community's anger and frustrations. It has been both hopeful and pessimistic. It has celebrated the beauty and myth of American exceptionalism and its special place in the world, while at the same time damning it to hell for not living up to the promises and ideals America espouses. It is a tradition that celebrates both the Creator or the Divine's hand in history—offering "hallelujahs" for deliverance from slavery and Jim and Jane Crow, while at the same time asking, "Where in the hell is God?" during tough and trying times. It is a tradition that develops a theological outlook quite different at times from orthodoxy—one that finds God very close, but so far away.[29]

BLM is thus a descendent of previous African American prophetic movements, in which people stand up and provide clarity and witness to the atrocities happening to Black bodies. Understood this way, the role of religion in social justice organizing does not limit the inclusivity of a movement, but rather is well-aligned with an intersectional analysis that seeks to uncover all of the many and varied ways anti-Black racism influences contemporary society.

"MY GOD IS BLACK. MY GOD IS FEMALE"

The founders of BLM may not have set out to begin an overtly religious movement, nor did most public scholars and pundits understand the movement through a lens of faith. Yet discussions of the movement reverberated with religious and spiritually based language, highlighting the ways Pentecostal piety and prophetic rhetoric often emerge within contemporary Black liberation movements as echoes and continuations of history. As some of our participants pointed out, many churches were deeply involved with BLM. One example was the invitation of a local pastor to the official BLM-Memphis organization to have their monthly meetings at his church. The reasoning behind this, according to Blair (African American, 21, Student), was so that "people on the street can come inside the church and participate in our meetings." In the tradition of the Black church's involvement with Black liberation, both through perspective and location, Blair shared that not only does the church offer its space free of charge, but additionally, the "Black Panther Party, Civil Rights Movement, NAACP, they all met at the churches, and that was our primary reason the Black Lives Matter Memphis chapter was to bring it back to . . . where we were all originated, and that's with the church." Here, Blair situates BLM in the historical narrative of previous Black liberation movements. For her, it does not matter that BLM started as a secular movement, devoid, as some would argue, of any religious or spiritual beliefs. For Blair, the work of BLM places it within the Black liberation tradition, inherently aligning it with the Black church.

Blair's explanation of BLM's church connection is rich with meaning, locating the movement spatially and foundationally within a religious setting. Not only did she locate the BLM-Memphis organization to those movements in the past, she clearly sees meeting at the church as a way to "bring it back, where we all originated . . . with the church." Two crucial points emerge from Blair's analysis. First, in announcing that she wants to "bring it back," she also infers that "it" had left. In the context of her answer, we argue that "it" was a movement that centered Black lives. She sees BLM creating the organization and apparatus to forge this new and continuing work, and she sees the role of the Black church as indispensable in helping BLM advocates to carry out this work.

Second, her answer infers that she sees the Black church as "originating" the type of activity in which she now locates an aspect of her identity. The church's location not only links BLM to a history of Black liberation, but it additionally speaks to the continuing struggles faced by Black people in Memphis and beyond. As she explains,

> meetings are geared towards [the church], so you bring people off the streets and into the community more. Let them know that, let's rebuild our city by creating unity within our communities, so to speak. So we, and its plus it's convenient because my church is right down the street from the [church] where our meetings are, so that was convenient from downtown to south Memphis instead of from downtown to East Memphis [which is at the opposite end of the city from downtown, and is primarily white and wealthier]. . . . A lot of our members live in Orange Mound and South Memphis and Whitehaven. So it was convenient for them, and some of them actually catch the MATA [public transit] bus to come to the meetings.

For Blair and BLM, this places them within a legacy of activism birthed from the church that bore witness to the issues germane to African Americans across a variety of places and times. By having meetings at a church, BLM can bring "people off the streets" to help "rebuild our city" by "creating unity" within communities. It is this recognition that placed Blair squarely within the tradition and connects her with activists throughout history and throughout time who forge these relationships. This analysis emphasizes the importance of linking individuals to communities, an idea at the center of Pentecostal piety and the history of social justice organizing.

We also argue that Blair's faith helps her in understanding that not all churches are part of this tradition. While some in her focus group criticized the church, she countered that criticism, largely by centering the Black church as a model for justice. While agreeing that the Black church has mimicked problems that people associate with organized religion, she suggests that those churches simply serve a "white god." Blair's faith, in contrast, is necessarily prophetic:

> My God is Black. My God is female, and God is a spirit of course, but my religion shouldn't oppress me. It should liberate me. It's like we fall into this trap believing white is right and . . . I don't understand, and it's like we, we just been white Christianity. That's what I call it. All these Black churches are white Christianity, and it's kinda hard for me to elaborate more because it's, it's really so confusing, cuz I'm still learning myself.

This personalization of a Black God for Blair should not come as a surprise. Throughout the history of African American religious thought, many thinkers have created the notion of a Black God. An example of this is the work of nineteenth-century African Methodist Episcopal (AME) Bishop Henry McNeal Turner. Johnson argues that when Turner preached "God is a Negro," Turner offered "a deep theological analysis on God-talk, language, and hermeneutics, in addition to providing a radical version of a contextual theology that predates our modern understanding of the term."[30] Additionally Turner "offers a critique of the hegemonic Christian interpretation of his day, asking African Americans to see and experience God in a new and affirming way."[31]

It is within this tradition that Blair experiences God. As with Turner's understanding of God, Blair's version responds to the contextual reality that she and other African Americans face, namely the problem of worshiping a God in which they cannot see themselves. Blair's interpretation reveals, as Turner argued, that "image is important and how one constructs God will have an impact on how a person sees herself or himself."[32] Moreover, as with Turner's "God is a Negro," we submit that Blair's understanding of God also functions as a "rhetoric of resistance." Vincent Wimbush reminds us that, "Resistance is necessarily a response to, and in its varied expressions partly determined by, the varied manifestations of power. The realm of the imaginary, the visionary, the utopic is discovered and cultivated by those who define themselves as pressed and limited in some significant ways by power, as a means of resisting such power."[33] This rhetoric of resistance—the assertion that God is a Black woman—also invites readers to see God as a "rhetorical construction, a site for contestation, or in rhetorical terms, a place of invention." Understanding God as a rhetorical construction also offers Blair a site of liberation because she is not only offering a different version and vision of God from the mainstream, but she also sees how this understanding ties into her own freedom and liberation. She understands that God stands with and for her because she too bears the image of God. Through this understanding of God as Black, Blair draws strength to resist white racist understandings of God and the faith, whether they come from white or Black churches.

While understanding God as Black is itself problematic in many circles, Blair's God is also female. That this framing represents a challenge to many in the Christian community is evidenced by the evangelical response to the bestselling novel *The Shack*.[34] In it, author William P. Young depicts God as a Black woman. The criticisms voiced by Mary Kassian, author of *The Feminist Mistake*, exemplify the response of many white Christians to the text:

> *The Shack* contains terribly wrong concepts about God. Plain and simple. If you think it doesn't, then you're well on your way to accepting the image of the Christa on the cross. In a few years, you'll be hanging her up in your church. I don't think I'm overstating the case. . . . The arguments used to justify their feminist Christa are the same ones *The Shack* uses to justify its feminized version of God. In essence, there's no difference between the artistic image of a feminized Jesus (a.k.a. "Sophia") hanging on a cross and the artistic image of a feminized Aunt Jemima Papa god in a book. If the latter doesn't offend you, then the former really shouldn't.[35]

When the film version of the book appeared years later, a Black woman depicting God was a bridge too far for some evangelicals. Though several evangelicals offered theological reasoning to obfuscate their disdain for a Black female God, Joe Schimmel, pastor of Blessed Hope Chapel in Simi Valley, California, was straightforward in his reasoning, noting the distinction he draws between "a heavy set, cushy, non-judgmental, African American woman called 'Papa'" and "the one true God revealed through the Lord Jesus Christ."[36] Calling the portrayal of God as a Black woman a "pretentious caricature," Schimmel illustrates the fierce reluctance to release God's image from the dominating rhetoric of the white evangelical church.

However, though Schimmel, Kassian, and other evangelicals claim the right to define God in their image, Blair is not alone in her reimagining of a Black female God. In Chicago artist Harmonia Rosales's rendering of the famous Sistine Chapel painting, the Creation of Adam, she reimagines both God and Adam as Black women. Some on Twitter called the artwork a "disgrace," "disgusting," and "cultural appropriation."[37] When interviewed about the piece she calls the Creation of God, Rosales said

We have been taught that God created "man" in his own image. [But] in fact, we have created God in our own image . . . I knew my transformation would draw attention to the statement I wanted to make, but the point here is to consider why we have accepted our historical representation of the beginning of life, of the Creator. . . . The original representation excludes something very important: women and people of color. I wanted people to consider creation through a different lens that, in turn, would cause us to consider the way we see everything else we have been taught to see. Perhaps it is time to rethink.[38]

Blair's reconceptualizing of her God illustrates the intentional nature of her connection with both religion and the BLM movement, in which she unapologetically shapes a counter-narrative to dominant teachings about God. Like Rosales's artwork, Blair's "Black" and "female" God questions "historical representations" of the Creator, creating a space of reinterpretation that invites people to rethink what they think they know about God. More importantly, though, the historically constructed God functions as a barrier, rather than a conduit, for Blair's call to activism. Central to her efficacy in social justice work is Blair's sense that God be Black and female, and that Blair herself be made in the image of God. God must affirm her features, image, and likeness. By articulating God, and consequently religion, in this way, Blair channels the strength she gains from her faith into her work against white supremacy, including her stance against Black churches who embrace white theology. Her centering God as the foundation of her interpretation of the faith allows her to keep her faith while simultaneously rejecting and renegotiating aspects that prevent her from realizing her capacity to promote social change. In so doing, she practices Pentecostal piety, allowing the Spirit to lead, shape, and give utterance to her motivations and actions.

"BLACK THEOLOGY MATTERS"

The renegotiation Blair performed, in which she understood herself as made in God's image and channeled that strength and energy into justice work, illustrates the importance of adapting theological views for the continued vibrancy of social movements. Emphasizing the historical role of religion in Black liberation, Martin (Black, 43, Activist) highlighted the role of the pastor and Black Churches during the civil rights movement. "Black pastors, preachers, and churches," he recalls, "finally got involved" in the civil rights movement. Echoing Blair's responses, Martin added that the minister's involvement also allowed the use of their churches to become "safe haven(s) to have meetings there, to have rallies there," and "to meet as a place for protesting." However, for him, the continued role of the church in providing support and energy for activists requires feedback between the movement and church leaders, and Black ministers who consequently shape the messages of the justice within their congregations. He explained,

> We gotta send a message out to Black preachers, Black pastors, and Black leaders in the community. We have to inform our people of what's going on. Because it's impossible to preach the gospel without being connected to the plight of the people. . . . Most of them (pastors) don't live in the community anyway. You preach in South Memphis (a predominately Black area), but you live in Collierville (a suburban city outside of Memphis). So you not hooked up to when Ray Ray got killed last night because he and a girl got into it, or the police shot him dead because he had a—some Skittles and a tea. So you can't even speak to that. So how can you offer pastoral counseling to a grieving mother in the midst of that, and you not there but two hours out of a week?

Martin's response is also part of the historical narrative of the Black Church. He sees the civil rights–era church not only as a place for rallies and protests, but also as the place where people gathered and shared information. For Martin, it is how the people stayed connected. However, the church is losing that connection because many of the pastors are no longer part of the community where they serve. This disconnect hurts not only the movement but also the ministry of pastoral counseling. Pastors who are disconnected cannot, in Martin's estimation, even speak to the realities that many of their "parishioners are going through."

Therefore, Martin's work with BLM centers the ideas that "Black theology matters," and as in Blair's analysis, the God of Black theology must be Black. "We're looking at the God for Black liberation right now," he told us, "so that's why we always refer back to the Exodus story. If we read more into the gospel, it's talking about us. It's talking about Jesus fighting for us, consistently. The poor people, the widower, the people who've been afflicted by government, terrorism, and things of that nature." For Martin, the foundation of (Black) theology must be a struggle for Black liberation. He grounds this thinking in the story of the Exodus, the biblical story of the freedom of the Israelites after their enslavement in Egypt, and in Jesus, who he interprets as fighting for the oppressed.

Martin's interpretation of God is not new. His theological foundation grounds itself in the work of theologian James Cone. From his seminal text, "Black Theology and Black Power,"[39] to his latest, *The Cross and the Lynching Tree,*[40] Cone has consistently articulated the idea that theology must speak to those who are suffering and oppressed in affirming ways. In short, the gospel must be one of liberation. Though Cone is a trained systematic theologian, Johnson calls him a "rhetorical theologian," one more concerned about how theology speaks and is understood by the people within a certain context.[41] It is Cone who first brought our attention to the fact that all theology is contextual and at its best, theology is a "soulful" enterprise as it "moves its audience to a better understanding of the Deity." In short, rephrasing rhetorical scholar Michael C. Leff and his understanding of rhetoric, Cone argues that theology is a contextual enterprise that finds its "habitation only in the particular."[42]

By understanding that theology is a contextual enterprise, or better, that God operates in contextual realities, this understanding can invite those who have questions about God, and to borrow Ganda's (African American, 35, Student/Research Assistant) phrasing, "what's really going on." Ganda came to the BLM movement through a sense of dissonance about white supremacist violence and her previous understanding of the Gospel:

> When I was younger, you know, I mean, you get older and wiser, and that's when you start to question things. So I think it's alright for me to be questioning; this is just not what I was taught that God created. . . . They took whatever they took—the gospel or whatever they did and twisted it and made it white supremacist—they made it fit the way that they needed it to fit. So like what do—so now what do we do? You know? You see the things where, oh, God couldn't have been the same, because this god here was the one—what about the slave master, and then you supposed to be worshipping the same god, or whatever.

For Ganda, the questioning of how religion should inform a situation of anti-Black violence led to a dissonance answered by protest and organizing for justice. Though Ganda's experiences with Black theology were more limited than Martin's, her sense, like Blair's, that faith could and should connect her with others who experienced similar forms of oppression and help them to find explanations for suffering and pathways toward change led her both to BLM and to a challenging of white theological framing of religion.

The question of alignment between faith and BLM were not always framed by renegotiation. Frank (Black, 37, Pastor), for instance, synthesizes "spirituality and scholarship" with his "social activism." He acknowledges and understands that his faith is an "inextricable part" of his orientation toward justice work, and therefore sees BLM as an "extension of my faith conviction." Kelly (African American, 48, Life Coach) said that an understanding of her faith and how God speaks and shapes her life continues to call her to speak up for justice. Sharing her experience of faith and the BLM movement as mutually constitutive, she told us,

> I think it's definitely an instance of my faith because I had a hard time trying to figure out what I wanted to do with my life and what I wanted to major in and I was like "oh my god I've changed my major four times," and I'm probably gone change again. But right now I'm like . . . I'd spoke with a woman, and she was like, "Girl you don't need to stress about what you wanna do. Do you know God don't care what you want to do, as long as you do what he tells you

to do and do everything you do in his name? Do it. And that's it. As long as
you do what you got to do for him and live for him every day, he doesn't care
what you want to do." So that means to me, I'm going to continue to say what I
have to say, I want to continue to speak up for what I believe is right and as
long as that pleases God, I'm pleased.

What Frank and Kelly highlight here is that their faith and work with
BLM also help them find the strength and energy to fight for their own and
others' rights. Frank practices this through scholarship, while Kelly channels
her religion convictions into a courage to speak up for what is right. In this
way, religion both brought people into the BLM movement, and the BLM
movement helped to reshape their theological orientation.

The idea that faith, race, and membership in BLM worked together to
energize and define one another is a key component of the religion rhetoric
of BLM members. Often participants articulated a "woke" understanding of
what religion could mean, defining faith as a historical component of Black
liberation that could and should adapt to contemporary concepts of change.
In this way, BLM and faith become identity components in the same ways
intersectional justice organizing considers gender, race, sexuality orientation,
and other axes of oppression and resistance. For Stella (Black, 37, Student/
Homemaker), her "faith," her "Blackness," and her "womanhood" is a
"package deal." She continued, "I'm a woman first before I'm anything else.
I wake up Black and a woman every day. So my feeling again is why do I
need to at any point separate my faith and why can't you figure out how to
have some and do justice because my faith calls for me to be socially involved, to be engaged with the community in which I live." As Stella's
testimony makes clear, faith motivated participants to get involved in Black
liberation, while at the same time prompting them to consider the ways their
faith can be informed by a socially just perspective.

A CHALLENGE OF ADAPTATION

The passionate reshaping of religious traditions and theology that conflict
with understandings of justice both illuminates the contemporary understanding of spirituality within BLM and highlights a common conflict between
white-dominated theology and Black liberation–based perspectives. While
the perspectives we have shared previously in this chapter reflect participants
who successfully renegotiated religion as mutually affirming to racial justice
activism, many BLM members resisted or fiercely critiqued organized religion. One of the major critiques by proponents of BLM is that the Church, and
particularly the Black Church, has been unresponsive to the atrocities happening to Black people. Alongside one atheist participant, several BLM affiliates in our study struggled to reconcile faith and a sense that the Church was

not adequately addressing injustice. For instance, while Chanel (Black, 28, Nonprofit Program Coordinator) described coming to BLM because of her "biblical worldview," she still "wrestled" with how the "Church and the idea of justice work together." Without articulating religion through a lens of Pentecostal piety and the prophetic tradition, Chanel and others were not able to fully reconcile their passion for justice with their connection to the Church. Here, the Black liberation tradition of the Church brought Chanel into BLM, but religion represented a site of dissonance for her identity within protest.

In other instances, the very tradition of prophetic rhetoric turned against churches themselves. For example, when Martin asked, "Why don't we see more Black pastors, civic leaders, preaching that Word and out here fighting for Black liberation?" Ganda had a quick answer. She remarked, "'Cause they so busy getting these poor Black people's money." Tensions like these highlight the ways that, even when Black liberation theology is dominant within activists' lives, the history of white supremacy within organized religion can remain dominant. Jermaine's (African American, 28, Teacher) analysis positions the previous role of the Black Church within the mid-twentieth-century civil rights movement against its contemporary lack of involvement. He described feeling "astonished" by the Church's current lack of influence, particularly given the strong role of the Black Church in history. In response to this remark, Dan (Persian/Caucasian, 24, Student) agreed, arguing,

> I think there's a big problem with getting churches involved . . . [because] churches have been used against Black people. Even if in America you have a lot of churches go together then you should expect that you'll have a lot of, for example, evangelicals in the Midwest that will create opposition . . . but unless that awakening is deeper in the Black culture, then it could be, it can be controlled and manipulated at any level by any form of opposition.

The awareness of racial oppression that not only infiltrated the Church through its members, but also that had historically worked against Black people through Church leaders, prompted Dan to identify as an atheist. Unlike Martin, Blair, and others, then, Dan's involvement within social justice activism prompted him to dissociate from the church, even while he realized the historical role of faith within civil rights organizing.

Dan's disillusionment with the Church is, of course, based on very real histories of racial oppression and white supremacy within many white Church traditions. Of the white people who spoke with us about their support of BLM, two had served as pastors within the white evangelical tradition. Like many of the Black congregants and pastors we spoke with, these white BLM affiliates were led by their faith to support the movement. For Tom (Irish American, 37, Student/Teacher/Minister), "Justice is at the heart of Christian faith." He told us that if he "finds out about injustice and I find out

about a way to act and speak for justice, and I have the means to participate . . . Time, money, other resources, whatever. Why wouldn't I? In my
view of biblical Christian faith, justice is at the heart. I guess it depends on
how you read the Bible. I wouldn't say it's the only thing at the heart, but it's
at the heart." It was a moment in which Tom saw an intersection between his
faith and BLM that led him to join the movement. Tom shared with us about
the time he preached on the subject of BLM:

> Last summer, I was scheduled to preach a sermon. We were going through a
> sermon series called "Glad you asked." We invited congregants to submit
> questions, and our preaching team took turns responding to the questions. I
> had a couple of sermons in the series, and one of them was, "How should
> Christians respond to racial tension?" I got selected for that one because I have
> some background with intercultural communications. That week was the
> church shooting in Charleston.

When asked whether this changed his sermon strategy, he replied that it
had, and that doing so posed a challenge within his very white, very conservative congregation. After the sermon, a congregant approached him to say
he "had gone too far and gotten too political." The man

> seemed to react most to a part towards the end of the sermon, where I was
> giving people practical things to do to . . . In response to how Christians have
> misused scripture to support racial injustice. He felt like I was lecturing to him
> about things that he felt like he didn't need to be lectured to about. He was
> speaking to me in love; I tried to listen in love. We're still friends, and he's
> still part of that church, and I was able to speak about racism again.

Several aspects of Tom's account reflect the theological struggles apparent in some BLM members' faith traditions. First, Tom's faith centers on
"justice," and since this is at the heart of his theological understanding, the
task for him is to discover places where injustice is taking place. Once this
happens, he feels called to "speak up" or "participate" in actions to help bring
attention to the injustice. In other words, it is Tom's vision for the ways his
previously held beliefs intersect with the BLM movement that drives him to
participate. Second, by saying, "I guess it depends on how you read the
Bible," he also infers that not all people see justice as a big part of the faith.
This is evident from the story he shares about preaching a BLM-themed
sermon. His experience of being criticized for portions of the sermon demonstrates the differences in biblical worldview in which some use the Bible to
support the movement and others to oppose it.

That Tom was confronted with accusations of being "too political" follows larger national patterns of public opinion, particularly among Christians. A widely cited study by the Barna Group showed that a majority of

White Christians (both evangelical and mainline) do not support the message of BLM.[43] Similarly, a majority of Americans believe that killings of African American men by police are isolated incidents, rather than part of a larger pattern of anti-Black violence.[44] This view is, unsurprisingly, amplified by race, with 65 percent of white people understanding police brutality as isolated incidents, but only 19 percent of Black people supporting this view.[45] Though we have argued that theology is justice-centered for many of our participants and others, white rejection of the idea of systemic anti-Black police violence is increased by religion. More than seven in ten white evangelical Protestants (72 percent), white mainline Protestants (73 percent), and white Catholics (71 percent) believe that killings of African American men by police are isolated incidents.[46] While a majority of white non-Christians also reject the systemic nature of police violence, these numbers are lower for the non-Christian religions (62 percent) and religiously unaffiliated Americans (59 percent).[47] This speaks volumes about Christian churches in America. While sharing the same faith as African Americans, white Christians are less inclined to believe their stories of violent policing than people who do not share their faith. At the same time, the Barna Study also showed that the overwhelming majority of Christians believe that "Christian churches play an important role in racial reconciliation."[48] For a majority of white Christians, then, "racial reconciliation" can only mean silence, not justice.[49]

A vision of "racial reconciliation," in which people seeking justice avoid getting "too political" and opt for silence rather than discomfort, was not only Tom's experience. Whereas Tom's faith led him to march and speak publicly, other white supporters of BLM felt more comfortable sharing their thoughts online; nearly identical motivations led different participants to join the movement in in-person or online forms, or to join both. When asked how respondents shared BLM information online, Martha (White, 30, Ministry) told us that most of her online posting has been "faith-related." She told us about the first time she remembered posting about BLM,

> was after the church massacre in Charleston. That prompted me to share my own story with all [one-]thousand of my Facebook friends, about my experience in racial conflicts and racial reconciliation within my own life, from the time that I was way younger, on. Within that, most of the prejudice that I had seen growing up came from within my church family. It was sharing that story and getting responses to that, including my grandpa's sister is like, "I hear what you're saying, but what about the thugs. Blah, blah, blah." I'm like, "You lost me at thugs because you clearly didn't hear anything that I said."

Just as Tom's previously held faith led him to join BLM for a march and share his convictions with his congregation, Martha's beliefs motivated her to post online. Her post was not an unthoughtful or shiftless click of a button, but rather a performance of her faith driven by observations and experiences growing up in the church. She went on to tell us that she directed her post to "white Christians," noting the ways white Christianity had been instrumental in the history of racial injustice. She suggested that white Christians "needed to respond and we needed to hear what people are saying. We need to be saying more about them." Like Tom, Martha was motivated to participate in the movement online through the intersection of her lifetime of faith with recent attention to racial reconciliation driven by BLM.

Demonstrating the ways online activism often crosses over into offline interactions, Martha's post prompted someone from her small group Bible study to engage her privately using the Inbox feature on Facebook. About the experience, she told us

> he was offended because I had directed it to white Christians and he was like, "This has been my experience. Black people need to also blah, blah, blah." I was like, "I didn't say that Black people don't need to do something, but I'm not a Black person, and the majority of my friends are white, on Facebook especially. I'm talking to you, not to anyone else." It was just this whole thing. Most of my responses have been prompted by faith-specific issues.

As an extension of her faith-driven participation in BLM, then, she saw individual conversations as part of her activism. Though she reported often using Facebook messenger to engage in the types of conversations she described above, she weighed this type of engagement against communicating at church:

> I only preach occasionally, and I have not yet flat out slammed it. I bring up bits and pieces, or I use stories as examples, but I'm not quite as direct in a sermon as I am in one-on-one conversations, or even on Facebook. I try to bring some, especially after seeing that. I try to bring some [racial justice analysis] into each sermon that I'm giving. I usually reserve the more direct [ideas] with one-on-one conversations. There's so much if you just pour it out and then just let people walk out the door. These are also people that I only see maybe once a month. I don't have any communication with them outside of that. I want to be able to follow up with people and talk with them more often.

Martha and Tom's stories are similar, not only in their faith-based motivation for participating in BLM, but also in their awareness of and experiences with potential negative effects. Like Tom, Martha faces backlash when offering support to her white friends and family. Also, like Tom, much of that resistance comes from members of their respective churches. They both are willing to talk to other white people about BLM and try to explain their support for the movement. In an ancient understanding of their faith, rooted in the spirituality of dialogue and a "faith seeking understanding,"[50] they are both willing to risk relationships, favor, being misunderstood, and ostracized for standing with and affirming BLM in part because they see the movement as an extension of their faith.

Moreover, grounded in their faith commitments, they feel that led to a move from just being "non-racist." As Jenn Jackson reminds us, "There's a big difference between the passive work of simply not being racist and the active work of dismantling systems of oppression."[51] That active work moves into the arena of being anti-racist. To be anti-racist is to go beyond being non-racist and actively engage in the dismantling of racist systems, ideas, and thoughts. This is what both Tom and Martha attempt to do, and for both of them, anti-racism is grounded in their faith and their preaching, protesting, and posting.

CONCLUSION

In this chapter, we examined the religious rhetoric of our participants and the connection between personal investments in faith, religion, or spirituality and participation in BLM. Despite being a secular movement, BLM is not void of spirituality or faith commitment. In fact, from the early days of the movement, people of faith stood bearing witness to and offering support for the atrocious violence that sparked the movement. As one BLM founder, Patrisse Khan-Cullors, notes, the work of the Spirit has been central in the movement generally and for her work specifically.[52] Khan-Cullors was not alone in her sense of connection between spirituality and the movement for Black lives. Many BLM affiliates felt called and lead by the "Spirit" to join in the movement and offer prophetic witness to the suffering and oppression of Black lives, a trend we explored through a lens of Pentecostal piety.

This connection speaks to the long tradition of Black Churches being involved in social justice issues and concerns, allowing many Black participants to understand the contemporary moment through both the religious foundation of civil rights history as well as their personal histories with the Church. Though many believed that Black Churches were not as active as they once were, many understood the tradition and the legacy of the civil rights movement and saw themselves as connected to the tradition of resistance through faith. The tradition gave our Black participants theological license to rethink, reshape, and reimagine what spirituality would look like in the BLM movement. This too, as we argued in this chapter, is part of the Black religious tradition. Born from the resistance to a narrative that told Black people that they were not created in the image of God, Black people always had to put forth narratives that not only included them but also reminded them that their lives matter.

Faith worked as an individual lens that allowed many to see their role in BLM as a continuation or renegotiation of civil rights history. This is a logical extension for participants with a connection to the Black Church, but it posed some challenges for white participants. As we have argued here, religion still functioned as the personal lens that united movement history with BLM, but in this case, the relationship was self-reflexive; BLM members who worshipped in white evangelical churches had to reexamine those traditions and find spiritual homes outside of the traditions. This speaks to the fact that a majority of white Christians simply do not affirm or understand BLM. Though most of them have a cerebral understanding of the theological doctrine of the imago Dei (the image of God), in practice, white evangelical Christianity has a legacy of racist and sexist ideologies and structures. Not only were some white Christians drawn to BLM through their religion, then, but their expressions of faith and spirituality were also shaped by the anti-racist, anti-sexist messages of the movement.

For participants of faith, BLM offered a way of understanding a personal relationship with spirituality as a bridge to past civil rights leaders. In this way, larger movement history worked to draw in new social justice participants implicitly through their individual connections to the Spirit. BLM is not an explicitly religious organization. Yet the history of Black liberation organizes bubbles beneath the movement for Black lives, emerging to offer a way in for Black and white Christians as well as those who understand faith through a more spiritual lens.

NOTES

1. Leah Gunning Francis, *Ferguson and Faith: Sparking Leadership and Awakening Community* (St. Louis: Chalice Press, 2015), 63–64.

2. Ibid., 64.

3. Ibid., 64.

4. Qtd. in Emily Sproul, "The Missing Gospel in Black Lives Matter," *Baptist News*, September 23, 2016, https://baptistnews.com/article/the-missing-gospel-in-Black-lives-matter/.

5. Ibid.

6. Emma Green, "Black Activism, Unchurched," *The Atlantic*, March 22, 2016, https://www.theatlantic.com/politics/archive/2016/03/Black-activism-baltimore-Black-church/474822/.

7. Adelle Banks, "Black Churches Are No Longer Ground Zero for Civil Rights Activism," *Religion News Service*, December 18, 2014, https://www.religionnews.com/2014/12/18/Black-churches-no-longer-ground-zero-civil-rights-activism/.

8. While we use the terms "religious rhetoric," "spirituality," and "faith," of our participants who self-identified as religious, 88 percent were Christian.

9. Lisa Robinson, "Some Honest Thoughts on #BlackLivesMatter, the Church and Real Reconciliation," *Lisa Robinson: Thinking and Living Theological Thoughts Out Loud*, May 13, 2016, https://theothoughts.com/2016/05/13/some-honest-thoughts-on-Blacklivesmatter-the-church-and-real-reconciliation/.

10. Ibid.

11. Anthony Bradley, "Black Lives Matter Doesn't Represent the Gospel, Nor Should It," *World*,   January   15,   2016,   https://world.wng.org/2016/01/Black_lives_matter_doesnt_represent_the_gospel_nor_should_it.

12. Christopher A. House, "Crying for Justice: The #BLACKLIVESMATTER Religious Rhetoric of Bishop T. D. Jakes," *Southern Journal of Communication* 83, no. 1 (2018): 1.

13. Ibid.

14. Ibid., 1.

15. Hebah H. Farrag, "The Role of Spirit in the #BlackLivesMatter Movement: A Conversation with Activist and Artist Patrisse Cullors," *Religion Dispatches*, June 24, 2015, http://religiondispatches.org/the-role-of-spirit-in-the-Blacklivesmatter-movement-a-conversation-with-activist-and-artist-patrisse-cullors/.

16. Ibid.

17. Farrag, "The Role of Spirit."

18. Elise Edwards, "'Let's Imagine Something Different': Spiritual Principles in Contemporary African American Justice Movements and Their Implications for the Built Environment," *Religions* 8, no. 12 (2017): 4.

19. Ibid.

20. Ibid.

21. Andrew Wilkes, "From Black Messiah to Black Lives Matter: How Pentecostal Piety Can Reveal the Charade of Racialized Capitalism," *The Guardian*, January 18, 2015, https://www.theguardian.com/commentisfree/2015/jan/18/black-messiah-black-lives-matter-pentecostal-piety-racialized-capitalism.

22. Ibid.

23. Andre E. Johnson, "Teaching in Ferguson: A Rhetorical Autoethnography from a Scholar/Activist," *Southern Communication Journal* 81, no. 4 (2016): 267–69.

24. Ibid.

25. Wilkes, "From Black Messiah."

26. Ibid.

27. Florian Horne, "Prophetic Witness in the News and as News," *Media Development* 59 no. 1 (2012): 57.

28. Ibid.

29. Andre E. Johnson, "'To Make the World So Damn Uncomfortable': W.E.B. Du Bois and the African American Prophetic Tradition," *Carolinas Communication Annual* 32 (2016): 22.

30. Andre E. Johnson, "God Is a Negro: The (Rhetorical) Black Theology of Bishop Henry McNeal Turner," *Black Theology: An International Journal* 13, no. 1 (April 2015): 29–40; 32.

31. Ibid.

32. Ibid.

33. Vincent L. Wimbush, "Introduction: Interpretating Resistance, Resisting Interpretations," *Semeia* 79 (1997): 1–10; 6.

34. See for example, "Six Major Problems with *The Shack*," *Leading the Way*, February 24, 2017, http://www.ltw.org/read/articles/2017/03/six-major-problems-with-the-shack.

35. Mary Kassian, "Re-imagining God in *The Shack*," *The Council on Biblical Manhood and Womanhood*, April 17, 2009, https://cbmw.org/uncategorized/re-imagining-god-in-the-shack/.

36. Heather Clark, "Christians Warn Upcoming Shack Movie Depicting God as Woman Could 'Far Outweigh' Harm of Novel," *Christian News*, December 20, 2016, http://christiannews.net/2016/12/20/christians-warn-upcoming-shack-movie-depicting-god-as-woman-could-far-outweigh-harm-of-novel/.

37. Raquel Laneri, "Uproar over Artist's Painting of God as a Black Woman," *New York Post*, May 30, 2017, https://nypost.com/2017/05/30/uproar-over-artists-painting-of-god-as-a-Black-woman/.

38. "This Artist Painted God as a Black Woman and Got a Lot of People Mad," *BET*, May 24, 2017, https://www.bet.com/style/2017/05/24/artist-goes-viral-with-black-woman god.html.

39. James Cone, *Black Theology and Black Power* (NY: Seabury Press, 1969).

40. James Cone, *The Cross and Lynching Tree* (Maryknoll, NY: Orbis Books, 2011).

41. Andre E. Johnson, "The Prophetic Persona of James Cone and the Rhetorical Theology of Black Theology," *Black Theology Journal* 8, no. 3 (2010): 266–85.

42. Michael C. Leff, "The Habitation of Rhetoric," in *Rethinking Rhetorical Theory, Criticism, and Pedagogy*, eds. Antonio de Velasco, John Angus Campbell, and David Henry (East Lansing: Michigan State University Press, 2016), 160.

43. Barna, "Black Lives Matter and Racial Tension in America," *Barna Group*, May 5, 2016, https://www.barna.com/research/Black-lives-matter-and-racial-tension-in-america/.

44. Robert P. Jones, Daniel Cox, Betsy Cooper, and Rachel Lienesch, "Anxiety, Nostalgia, and Mistrust: Findings from the 2015 America Values Survey," *Public Religion Research Institute*, November 17, 2015, https://www.prri.org/wp-content/uploads/2015/11/PRRI-AVS-2015.pdf.

45. Ibid.

46. Ibid.

47. Ibid.

48. Barna, "Black Lives Matter and Racial Tension in America."

49. We do not support the idea of racial reconciliation. As Johnson has noted elsewhere, "reconciliation can truly happen only if the people had a relationship together in the first place. What I mean by this is that reconciliation is about two parties coming BACK together and restoring their relationship. In short, if there was never a relationship in the first place, reconciliation cannot happen. Thus, when we speak of racial reconciliation, we ASSUME that the 'races' had a relationship that was healthy and wholesome at one time." Andre E. Johnson, "The Fallacy of Racial Reconciliation," *Rhetoric, Race, and Religion Blog*, March 16, 2018, http://www.patheos.com/blogs/rhetoricraceandreligion/2018/03/fallacy-racial-reconciliation.html.

50. "Faith seeking understanding" was the motto of Anselmo d'Aosta, better known as Saint Anselm of Canterbury, an eleventh-century philosopher and theologian of the Catholic Church. While philosophers, theologians, and religious studies scholars have debated Anslem's meaning of the phrase, it is commonly understood to mean "an active love of God, seeking a deeper meaning of God." See Saint Anselm, *Stanford Encyclopedia of Philosophy*, https://plato.stanford.edu/entries/anselm/#FaiSeeUndChaPurAnsThePro.

51. Jenn Jackson, "Doing the Work: White People Must Invest in Anti-Racism," *Bitch Media*, December 26, 2017, https://www.bitchmedia.org/article/white-people-invest-in-anti-racism.

52. Patrisse Khan-Cullors, Interview by Deborah Small, *The Root*, January 8, 2018, https://www.theroot.com/Black-womens-lives-matter-a-discussion-with-blm-co-fou-1821866044.

Chapter Four

"We're Killing People at an Astronomical Rate"

#ALM, Postracialism, and the Politics of Fear

In May 2016, we sat down to talk to Bob (50, White, Salesman). While we had spoken with eight groups of BLM advocates over two months by that point, Bob was the first to agree to speak with us about his support of #ALM, after we opened participation up to include one-on-one interviews. During Bob's interview, and in the others that followed, it became very clear why discussions of #ALM needed to be private—it felt as though the participants saw the interview as a therapy session. Getting increasingly emotional and repeating himself several times, Bob revealed to us how disposable he felt. "Just like that plastic cup on your desk," he said three times. He worried about neighbors and family members turning on him. Later, we spoke with Steve (58, White, Locksmith), who similarly revealed he was losing touch with his son. Jesse (25, White, Self-employed Handyman) recounted stories of being bullied as a child and of the ways seeing his own son bullied brought his pain flooding back to the surface. In each of these cases, the detail and level of transparency about past life events, fears, and insecurities was strik-ing. In cases like these, we were unsettled by the way these participants seemed desperate to share their stories with someone who would listen. Responding to questions like "What does #ALM mean to you?" these partici-pants poured out their most traumatic memories, often with a tenor of shame.

The context manifested in such impromptu confessionals is one that is both lacking intimacy and overflowing with fear. Ruth Wodak credits the horrific events of 9/11 as a turn that solidified the contemporary culture of fear.[1] While certainly press coverage of 9/11 and other large-scale events exacerbates a cultural sense of foreboding, as Susan Smith and Rachel Pain write, "Fear does not pop out of the heavens and hover in the ether before blanketing itself across huge segments of cities and societies; it has to be lived and—crucially—made" through constantly playing and replaying horrific and traumatizing events in news media, social media, and in daily interaction.[2] These fears are not purely constructed. If they were fabricated and demonstrably false, they might be more easily disbanded. Instead, cultural fears related to terrorism, environmental disaster, random violence, disease epidemics, and other modern catastrophes contain just enough truth to render them sticky.

Running alongside the culture of fear is a contemporary moment of racial awareness for many white Americans who had fully subscribed to postracialism as a moral stance. By postracialism, we refer to the often well meaning but always misguided idea that race and racism are no longer relevant concepts, and that American society has moved beyond their impacts. Postracialism and the culture of fear have been comfortable companions for decades, appearing at least as early as the 1960s, in the midst of the Vietnam War and massive civil rights organizing, and fiercely resurfacing in public consciousness with the election of America's first Black president.[3] As Wodak writes, it is no coincidence that massive right-wing fear of policies involving "economic, security and health care policies" coincided with Barack Obama's election. For some Americans, an Obama presidency represented the intense fear of the Other in power, both through the promise of liberal policies and the end of a string of forty-three white presidencies. This moment not only invoked fear in some (mostly white) Americans; it also signified for others an end to the barriers that prevented Black men from attaining power. Thus, a cultural context emerged in which fear and postracialism lived side by side.

In this chapter, we argue that #ALM represents the eruption of postracialism and the cultural politics of fear. For our participants, fear was a primary motivation for identifying with #ALM, as they understood the world to be increasingly dangerous. Since these cultural fears were fragmented and abstract, participants sought a concrete object of blame. While most participants believed in BLM's mission, they simultaneously found blame in BLM's focus on Blackness, an internal contradiction that only becomes legible in a postracialist context; our #ALM participants read BLM's centralization of race as a type of discursive violence, leading them to push back against the movement even while they ostensibly supported many of its goals. By approaching #ALM as the junction of fear and postracialist politics, we demonstrate the concrete ways these converging discourses contribute to a reinvestment in postracialism that actually exacerbates cultural fear and danger, particularly those that necessitated BLM in the first place.

THE "POSTRACIAL" CONTEXT

#ALM's emergence becomes legible only in the context of two converging cultural moments: postracialism and a climate of cultural fear, two moments that apparently connect to Barack Obama's presidency. Following the 2008 election, reports widely circulated that many Democratic voters paid little or no attention to Obama's race when casting their votes. This reporting was used to connect the Obama presidency with the dawn of a new postracial era.[4] Positioning the presidency as the ultimate office of U.S. power, Kent Ono writes, such arguments reason "that a Black man became the president of the United States implies that past racial barriers to occupying that office are now gone."[5] Consequently, subscribers to postracialism understand racism as a historical relic, rendered illegible by the perhaps well-intentioned but generally unhelpful insistence that they "don't see race."[6]

Many who insist on colorblindness were less optimistic about Obama's presidency. As Eduardo Bonilla-Silva points out, colorblindness did not emerge with Obama's presidency, but rather has historically intensified alongside social movements, beginning at least as early as the mid-1960s.[7] Just as the civil rights movement faced a fierce, often violent countermovement, Obama's presidency also coincided with the rise of groups like the Tea Party, who seemed to strike out not only "in reaction to a 'Black man' sitting in the White House,"[8] but also under the general fear that the world was changing, and not for the better. For some, it might be reasoned, the purported loss of racial categories championed by postracialism mimicked the disintegration of reassuring social structures; by "not seeing race," postracialist logics challenge the maintenance of segregated racial spaces in everyday culture and in America's highest office.

While Obama may have evidenced a postracial era for some, postracialism is a product of its context. Set against a backdrop of increasing percentages of incarcerated women and men of color, Obama's presidency marked a deeply troubling incongruity that held up the accomplishments of an individual Black politician against systems of continuing racism.[9] Sarah Banet-Weiser describes the current cultural moment as one of ambivalence, in which consumers understand the economic and political contexts of identity as both contradictory and natural.[10] This situation, of holding seemingly conflicting discourses simultaneously, is mirrored in the ways digital citizens approach race. As Nakamura and Chow-White argue, the saturation of technology into discussions of identity supports a "techno-genetic turn" in which we discuss race through the lens of phenotype, moving cultural discussions about race away from the socio-historical and into the pseudo-objectivity of science and technology.[11] By erasing history and collective experience, postracialist arguments take on deeply ambivalent meanings, as what should be and what is are often framed as individual identity issues rather than oppressive systems.

Situated in the ambivalent context Nakamura and Chow-White call "the paradox of race after the Age of the Internet," postracialism contains three primary components: the belief that racism is over, the proposition that people of color can and should adopt invisible racial identities, and the rhetoric of individual liberties to justify white supremacist violence.[12] First, postracialism centralizes the "sincere fiction" that racism no longer exists in the United States.[13] Assertions that the country has moved beyond the "icky historical abomination known as racism" take numerous forms ranging from multicultural tolerance pledges to rationalizations that even historical claims of racism were overblown.[14] This idea that racism is negligible and historical also emerges in claims of "reverse racism," as many (mostly white) Americans espouse the belief that discussing racism in public discourse equates to "thinking about the past."[15]

Second, postracialism demands "colorblindness" as a racial identity. Oliver calls this use of colorblindness a "hysterical symptom" that represses racial difference in public discourse.[16] This strategy aims to provide white Americans immunity from racism by claiming an inability to see race.[17] Of course, as Michael Eric Dyson points out, colorblind ideology asks much more of citizens of color than it does of white Americans; standing in opposition to the post- or antiracist goals of dismantling oppressive systems, postracialism instead asks Black and brown Americans to "delete crucial strands of our identity" for white comfort.[18] Postracialism attributes racism to divisions between races, rather than white supremacist structures. Colorblindness thereby holds up racism by imagining away the visible evidence of racial inequity and the socio-historical meanings of racial markers, while perpetuating the mechanisms of systemic racism.[19] Colorblind ideology asks Americans of color to give up their racial identities and instead "identif[y] with the very systems and people who would kill them without a second thought."[20] Colorblindness, in other words, urges acceptance of white supremacy by reasserting invisible whiteness as the only acceptable norm.

Third and finally, postracialism appeals to individual liberties as a way of distancing racial violence from white supremacy's systemic nature. The dominant discourse used to justify maintenance of racially biased systems, Bonilla-Silva writes, is an appeal to liberalism.[21] By imagining all Americans have the same opportunities for success, an assertion belied by copious evidence of racial disparities in education, housing, employment, and other vital areas, postracialism insists that failure is the fault of the individual. This "new racism," as Patricia Hill Collins calls it, is so preoccupied with individual liberties that it obfuscates continued systemic violence and inequality.[22] Like the other tenets of postracialism, the focus on individualism is couched in "a veneer of goodwill";[23] while it purports to uplift racial progress through nods to diversity, the individual focus succeeds by labeling examples of racism, from microaggressions to police brutality, as "isolated incidences."[24] Thus, by distancing such occurrences from larger patterns, postracialism forecloses the possibility of dismantling white supremacy.

These three interwoven tenets of postracialism reinforce existing systems of racial inequality by pretending racism is historical, mislabeled, and individual. Postracialism resists claims of racism's deleterious effects while simultaneously unraveling progressive gains of the late twentieth century and emboldening systemic racism.[25] Though discourses similar to postracialism began at least as early as the late 1960s,[26] Obama's 2008 election increased public support for this ideology to the detriment of anti-racist discourse, organizing, and scholarship.[27]

THE FORCE OF FEAR

Particularly for the political right, Obama's election represented a culmination of years of fear-based politics. As Smith and Pain argue, the attacks of September 11 upset "the spatial politics of fear" as concerns over unknown foreign entities manifested within the United States.[28] Emboldened by the 2001 attack, the Bush administration called for an investment in patriotism marked by an unquestioning acceptance of governmental action.[29] This call to patriotism demonstrates Sara Ahmed's contention that individual liberty and fear are often deployed in tandem in contemporary politics.[30] Placing citizens' fears of real, dangerous events in conversation with governmental rhetoric repositions freedom as "the freedom from fear."[31] Ahmed's discussion illustrates Smith and Pain's double helix model for fear's relationship to rhetorics of terror.[32] In their model, the geopolitical and the everyday are connected through strands of experiences, discourses, and observations. These connections are delicate but stable: "The breaks and discontinuities that occur—both randomly and in patterned ways—might represent the awkward, unfinished, disunited, conflicting nature of relations between the geopolitical and the everyday; but ultimately they are inter-reliant and complementary."[33] In this way, the politics of fear tethers large, abstract messages of danger to immediate experiences of harm, and the resulting double helix can be harnessed for political gain.[34]

Central to Smith and Pain's model is the acknowledgment that fear grows from real events, making fearful responses stubborn.[35] As Nicol writes, fear is often understood through "a misleading opposition between real and threatened danger," a position that involves the dismissal of some fears as less worthy than others.[36] Ahmed and others caution us about trivializing fears we do not share, noting that fears of women and people of color often emerge from experiential and historical violence.[37] These fears restrict movement and discourse in the public sphere. We add that the uncritical dismissal of deeply felt fears can actually compound those fears; in learning that their fears are not taken seriously, a frightened person also discovers there are no allies who will protect them from or fight back with them against the object of fear. When the object of fear is a real threat, as in the cases of police brutality, domestic violence, sexual assault, or gun violence, such isolation "delimit[s] movement in the public, and over-inhabitance in the private."[38] When the object of fear is in fact a harmless person, this sense of fearful isolation results in micro-aggressions at best and vigilantism at worst. As an emotion, fear is both affective and cognitive, influenced by experience, belief, and sensation. As such, Gil notes, we read fear through the same lenses we use to read the world in general, often overestimating or underestimating the real threat posed in various situations.[39]

While more abstract fears may seem less reasonable, dispersed threats are actually more destabilizing. To alleviate fear, we are driven to concretize threat as a particular person, thing, or group. Ahmed poses a challenge to Heidegger's assertion that fear objects can be handled by simply removing the stimulus.[40] Instead, a tangible fear object paradoxically offers some comfort since it is identifiable and therefore contained; in fact, the object's exit from our sensory field makes it all the more frightening for its promise of eventual return.[41] Our urge for containment explains a great deal about the ways fear has been harnessed historically. Wodak notes fear appeals work through the suggestion of real, tangible scapegoats, often reified in various minority groups, that can be blamed and purged in service of fear.[42] The effect of such moves is cyclical, since the creation of scapegoats separates us into in-groups and out-groups which distances communities from potential allies.[43] Isolating "those who are 'under threat' and those who threaten,"[44] Ahmed argues, itself produces fear, so we constantly seek a reified, containable threat.[45]

The nature of fear forecloses the possibility of protecting ourselves from it; while fear exists in the present as real, felt emotion, Ahmed points out that fear is always the anticipation of future suffering.[46] As Goodman argues, attempts to protect against threat often result in fear themselves.[47] In signaling the approach of a threat, a siren, for example, creates fear, manufacturing in us the "edginess, nervousness, or the jitters" that mark the affective dimension of fear.[48] This effect is even more pronounced in cases of amorphous threats such as fear of crime.[49] Just as fear announces itself through a statement of being afraid, fear can also contribute to the development of our particular subjectivity.[50] As Gil argues, fear can operate as the imaginary anticipation of a threatening situation . . . if a person develops a faint-hearted character, she will be prone to think that many things are dangerous, even if they are not; similarly, fear can be induced by others when something is represented as dangerous, even if the danger is not real.[51]

In this way, the future-facing position of fear recreates the possibility of fearful subjects, since the act of looking forward to possible threats creates the uncertainty fear needs to thrive. Fear, then, must be understood as anticipation that is managed, most often, by investing in particular entities as potential threats. As such, fear becomes a powerful motivator for the organization and governance of communities and cultures as variant as BLM and #ALM.

We agree with scholars like Ahmed and Bonilla-Silva that the "culture of fear" and postracialism, respectively, are not entirely new phenomena.[52] Yet in "the Age of the Internet," these discourses spread in ways unique to social media's possibilities and limitations.[53] Kettrey and Laster remind us online communication reflects users' offline identities.[54] The publics users form through engagement in online communication, and we add offline communication about online activities, parallel the structures of public organization experienced in everyday life.[55] Therefore, scholars should be attuned to the convergence of cultural threads in online communication. In the case of #ALM, we argue, discourses of postracialism and fear converge in a single hashtag. However, despite efforts to decode the meanings of this hashtag through the posts themselves, the #ALM advocates we interviewed reflected not only a more complex set of motivations, but also a more diverse set of identities.

#ALM AND THE CULTURE OF FEAR

We did not question our participants about their fears. Rather, detailed and sometimes jarring discussions of fear emerged from questions about their uses and understandings of #ALM. The entanglement of worldviews and anticipated threats follows Gil's contention that we interpret threat levels based on our understanding of particular environments and contexts.[56] As Freeden explains, "Menace may be clothed in the universal form of the threat to harm, but the cultural content of what constitutes harm and what triggers fear will both vary and converge."[57] As our participants described their reasons for preferring #ALM to BLM, they revealed much about their sense of insecurity and danger in the contemporary world, their prioritization of threat, and the translation of fear into and through postracialist ideologies.

For many of the #ALM users we interviewed, the danger of the modern world manifested in horrific threats to children. Brenda (67, White, Retired business owner), for example, explained the horrors of Palestinian child soldiers she had seen on Facebook, noting, "They take the children and they teach 'em—four years old—how to shoot guns, how to behead." Though in

Brenda's case, this post was not explicitly related to #ALM, a video that resonated with Jesse (25, White, Self-employed) was; as a former victim of bullying who now has a school-aged son, he connected with a Facebook video about an autistic child who was bullied for his disability. Describing the video with an intense level of affective detail, Jesse told us the bullied child

> [S]tayed in a closet in a dark corner a real long time, just sittin' there cryin' and huggin' his teddy bear . . . because he thought that was the only person he could come to. And then by the time it was over with, this child literally killed himself.

Like Brenda, Jesse understood this problem as systemic and widespread, noting that the topic of bullying "popped up in All Lives Matter . . . we need to stop this before it gets too bad." Jesse's post is also key in that his online post also connected to real-life experiences, illustrating Ahmed's "relationships of proximity."[58] Not only is his fear based on the perception of, or real life, proximity to danger, but this sense of being connected to danger also drove Jesse's posting. In other words, his motivation for participating in #ALM was his sense that the hashtag spoke to his previous experiences. Similarly, Tasha (37, Black, Teacher) worried that "in different parts of the city or even on Facebook cause I'm on there a lot, I've seen children holding guns," and in the most horrific example we heard, Beth (56, Black, Retired), a former CPS worker, recalled, "I've had children in my arms that have had hot curling irons stuck up their rectum." In each of these cases, we noticed the urgency with which participants communicated the harms befalling children locally and globally. Such urgency was, in these cases, likely a result of the participants' experiences working with children in their careers. Putting these issues either before or alongside the issues raised by BLM advocates seemed natural to them since the horrors they described impacted children, a group they encountered and advocated for every day.

#ALM advocates also worried about violence that might befall them or their family members, often speaking from their own experiences. Recalling his church-organized nursing home volunteer work, Bob (50, White, Salesperson) decried what he saw as a "disposable" society: "We're at the point right now that if you can become a certain age, we're tired of fooling with ya. We're gonna pull the plug, we're tired of fooling with ya." Through poor elder care and abortion, Bob believed, "we're killing people at an astronomical rate." Beth spoke from her experience watching her mother's abuse at the hands of "every man she's been with, you know, she's had a lot, she's had to have her problems in the past," noting that she preferred #ALM to BLM because it "cover[s] domestic violence." Tasha feared that "we can be on campus right now, go outside and have our purse snatched and we try to hold onto it we can die right there." These accounts that place death close to the self and family illustrate Ahmed's discussion of the ways fear restricts movement, drawing threat's proximity closer.[59] The sense that danger and violent threat lurked just beyond their current physical position in society encouraged further shrinking from, and thereby intensifying, external threats. Bob, for example, believed our society had devolved from actual communication, noting "if my neighbor looks at me funny or he said something and I didn't know how to take it, I'm gonna blow his head off. I'm gonna punch his lights out." Shelby (52, White, Physical Therapist) mourned the November 2015 terrorist attacks in Paris, worrying that "we've got a lot of real enemies out there," and Athena (27, White, Self-employed) questioned, "Who are we to finish God's work in killing each other?" In each of these examples, participants worried that they faced real threats in the world, either locally or nationally, and the connection they understood between their real lives and the things they saw associated with #ALM motivated them to engage and spread #ALM's rhetoric. Just as their fears for children drove them to advocate for a broader approach to mattering lives, their fear for their lives and their families represented tangible, though unpredictable, threats within American society that usurped the fears of police violence driving BLM and drove them to #ALM affiliation.

Our participants' concern with violence and social destruction led them to advocate for unity and equality through #ALM; in many instances, they were arguing for the same end goals common to BLM. Brenda believed that #ALM participants "all want the best for everybody" and told us she had "not heard anything negative about All Lives Matter." This goal of positive change connects to issues of race, Ashley (26, Black, Waitress) told us, because "[we] want to get rid of racism. So, the way that we get rid of racism is equality for all. Everybody matters." Tasha agreed with this perspective, noting, "I don't care what color you are, what religion, . . . [because] everybody is loved by somebody." Ashley and Tasha's nods to love illustrate Ahmed's contention that fear is amplified by our urge to shelter ourselves in the safe and familiar.[60] However, just as our participants' concerns were broader than racial injustice, their hopes for social change were also more general than racial equality. Referencing issues of class, Allie (57, Black, Retired) remarked, "I might be poorer that you, but . . . in the eyes of the Lord, we're all equal," and connecting #ALM to age, Bob told us "every single life—whether it be the five-year-old, six-year-old, the one-year, the unborn, the 95-year-old—all of their lives matter." Fear, here, extends "the fantasy of love as the preservation of life," under the guise that retreating into love and kindness shields us from threat.[61] Indeed, these fears were put into conversation with our participants' own experiences of bias; as Erykah (36, Black/Native, Massage Therapist/Artist) urged, "Don't think because I look a certain way, I feel a certain way, or you look a certain way I think you feel a certain way. Let's just treat everyone how you want to be treated." Our participants seemed to translate what we understood as intense fear for those they felt were most subject to injustice into a desire for protective love. In some cases, participants were concerned with issues that were not necessarily widespread, but they were genuinely invested in shielding victims of injustice.

In our conversations about instances of injustice and violence, participants referenced a desire for social unity driven by the perception that the country was becoming more divided. They sought postracial unity, which was their understanding of cultural love, as a shelter from fear. Following Obama's election, Athena believed "there was more Black people that stood up and said, 'we have power now, we can voice anything.' Feeling like they have to be segregated, that they had more power over white people, Chinese people, whatever people." Echoing this sentiment, Ashley remarked, "Isolating people from people and separating people off by racial backgrounds and things like that. . . . We're gonna end up self-destructing. We're gonna kill ourselves. We're gonna destroy ourselves with, you know, this group hate thing." Ashley's comment here is revealing in its definitions of love and death: love, here, is a unity that requires colorblind racial performance, while death is a result of resisting that postracialist outlook. Fear, then, is both an obstacle to love and the result of disunity. To follow Ahmed's argument that fear arises from the threat of loss, these threats seem to arise as much from the loss of postracialist ideology as they do from impending harm.[62] While participants worried about the impacts of segregation, #ALM gave them hope that the country as a whole was ready for unity. Bob felt that "the country's looking at this going, 'Stop with the separation. Stop dividing people,'" and Shelby urged the country to "stop looking at ways to separate us and maybe find ways to bring us together." In a comment that syntactically echoed Trump's campaign slogan, Derek (31, Black, Teacher) hoped "we all can work together and, like, make America back whole again." For these participants, many of whom were "taught from a very young age that we are all one in this country" (Pat, 57, White, Marketing Director), the movements for social justice reflected a dangerous precedent of divisiveness that threatened to take the country "down the tubes" (Pat).

Many of our interviews were intense, as #ALM advocates seemed to grow overwhelmed and distraught from the horrors of the world. They saw violence on social media and in their city, and they desperately wanted to solve these problems. We might respond to these fears by noting the staggering number of videos depicting police killings of unarmed Black men over the past several years; certainly, those videos are violent and fear-inducing too. However, our participants identified with issues more varied and less defined, as with the general threats of terrorists, purse snatchers, and violent children. Ahmed positions love as opposite fear, so that a "loved object" stands in as a "home or enclosure" that promises to protect us from the object of fear.[63] Important here is her point that the object of love need not be an object that actually promises love; in fact, the loved object may actually reject our advances. Moreover, the loved object can itself be completely imaginary and unbounded. In these cases, Ahmed writes, the fear itself allows us to "contain that which cannot be."[64] In the case of #ALM, we suggest, participants' wide-ranging fears allow them to more clearly imagine a postracial society that promises themselves and others protection. This postracial panacea is reified in #ALM. Because the fears imagined to be solved by #ALM connect so deeply to participants' everyday perceptions and experiences, they are motivated to join in the communal rhetoric of #ALM.

#ALM'S POSTRACIALIST DOCTRINE

That colorblind ideologies have been circulating for at least half a century indicates a well-established cultural context of postracialism.[65] Many of our participants were raised to believe they are not supposed to see race and that they should be inclusive and promote diversity. This belief, then, prompts them to advocate for equality not by advocating for a particular group, like BLM, but only through advocating for equality as a general and abstract idea. In our interviews, this emerged through outlining the other types of lives that should matter equally to Black lives. Explaining his contention that much of the country agreed with #ALM's viewpoint, Bob remarked:

> As America is looking at that and going, "Wait. Stop. Yes, Black lives matter. Indian lives matter. Chinese lives matter. Hispanic lives matter. White lives matter. Ladies' lives matter. Men lives matter. Little boys—nine-year-olds matter. Seventeen-year-olds matter. Ninety-five-year-olds matter. All lives matter. Why are we separating ourselves, saying your particular segment matters?" So somebody asks you, "Do you agree that with all Black lives matter?" Well, yes. And carry this down further: all lives matter.

Though some might argue that Bob's support of #ALM works to undercut BLM, he claims to support BLM. Max (19, Black, Receptionist), too, repeatedly emphasized his support of BLM, but also reported believing in #ALM as a broader movement for the value of life: "It's just a broader concept of BLM. Just like, Asian lives matter, Latin lives matter. You know, Women rights matter. So, it just depends on the issues that's going on." Erykah also supported BLM alongside #ALM, noting that she had used #ALM specifically to advocate for LGBT rights as well as deaths in other racial communities. She explained, "Black lives matter, simple fact. Hispanic lives matter, simple fact. You know, LGBT lives matter, simple fact." Projecting the emphasis of BLM on police brutality onto other racial groups, Diamond (34, Black, Retirement Specialist) advocated that "anyone that's brutalized by the police, not just African-Americans but anyone, no matter what their race, creed and color" should see justice served. In each of these examples, our participants emphasized the necessity of advocating for lives beyond the Black community at times, even while they ostensibly support BLM. As Allie told us, "All lives should matter, regardless of who you are. It doesn't matter whether I've got three eyes, or four noses. It doesn't matter. Your, their lives matter. They're somebody's child." Listing these many varieties of people works, Oliver writes, to construct a fantasy world.[66] In this case people with many noses or eyes stand in for the common conjuring of not caring "whether he is Black, white, green, or purple," an image that displaces meaningful conversations about contemporary racial inequalities into an imaginary world.[67] Indeed, the idea of people with multiple noses is in many ways as imaginary as a world in which race does not matter, and the conjuring of many alternative interest groups oppositional to BLM serves the same distracting purpose.

This attitude of advocating beyond BLM through what they believed to be inclusiveness also came through in how they defined the meaning and purpose of #ALM. Steve saw #ALM as:

> [A] supplement [to BLM], because it provides another opinion, which is important . . . if you watch the news to develop a balanced viewpoint, you may want to watch Fox News and you may want to watch MSNBC . . . I think it's important to pay attention to both.

This sentiment, that #ALM did not harm or take away from the message of BLM but rather provided balance to the movement, was common among our participants. For some participants, this meant that #ALM rendered BLM moot, as when Jesse told us "technically we're still covering the bases on [BLM's] subject, through All Lives Matter." Robert (21, Black, Material Handler), too, noted that "all is one works better than separating. You can stop one group of people. When it's a lot of groups of people, [that] works better for all the groups of people [working] together." Others, though, were clear that #ALM was not meant to negate BLM. Erykah, for example, told us she had used #ALM "with the [Paris] bombings . . . and LGBT community. I used it for those, to support issues outside of Black Lives Matter." She then clarified, "I didn't want any confusion as to thinking that it was the opposite of supporting Black Lives Matter." Erykah's ambivalence, of supporting BLM and #ALM but realizing that most people did not see the two as compatible, was common as participants articulated their support of #ALM and BLM. Articulating this ambivalence, Max told us the goal of #ALM is:

> [T]o broaden the prospective of people saying Black Lives Matter and try to include statistics of other people and how all lives matter. I guess that's positively the intended goal. But negatively, I just kind of see in social media with

All Lives Matter is just a combat once again on how the Black Lives Matter movement shouldn't be.

In these responses, we sense ambivalent inclusiveness; most of our participants seemed to have a clear understanding of the goals of BLM and were generally supportive of those goals. At the same time, they seemed to feel some hesitation or guilt about excluding others, particularly other people of color, from this important movement.

Through the ambivalence of advocating for both BLM and #ALM, our participants leaned on ideologies of colorblindness common to postracialism. Shelby, for example, remembered hearing "we all matter, so all lives matter . . . I don't remember exactly when I first heard it, but [that] seemed like a natural response." So common is this idea of colorblindness as a movement toward equality and unity, Shelby described it as "natural." Bob, too, advocated for an understanding of race that ignores divisions, noting, "There is only one race. And that's the human race." These responses illustrate the ways seemingly liberal discourses about diversity and multiculturalism are turned against people of color who highlight issues of racism.[68] Athena illustrated this sentiment when she told us most people "just see Black and white. They don't see . . . God is of every color." Bonilla-Silva notes that many white Americans believe racism is only a problem because people of color refuse to stop talking about it.[69] While this sentiment was much more common among White participants, Ashley shared a similar sentiment. Noting that she had never felt "that a person was looking down on me just because I'm Black," she recounted a conversation with her son in which she told him:

> I want to teach you that all lives matter . . . I don't want you to go to a school to where it's all Black people and you get this idea in your head that, you know, Black, Black, Black, Black, Black. I don't want to shove that on you. I want you to have empathy for everybody. I want you to identify with everybody. We're all human. We're all people.

Derek asserted a similar concern about "driv[ing] a wedge between races," and described #ALM's approach to race as "want[ing] to try and fix something that's already almost broken." These responses indicate the strong influence of postracialism that position colorblindness as a panacea for social ills. In such a context, the argument that it is actually racism and white supremacist violence that separates Americans has no salience, since these arguments are rooted in the "hysterical symptom" of not seeing color.[70] Instead, arguments about the unity of the human race were more persuasive for our participants, leading them to advocate for #ALM. For many participants and for many Americans in general, colorblind postracialism has so completely saturated public discourse that it cannot be easily dismissed.

SEARCHING FOR A POSTRACIALIST OBJECT OF FEAR

Believing that #ALM was a necessary antidote for a segregated society, our participants blamed BLM for the divisiveness they saw around them. Athena stated this explicitly, calling BLM "segregated that way. It's not as diverse. It makes them look stuck up and snooty. . . . Like, we don't care about you, we care about our kind." For Beth, too, "If you stop at Black life matters, I'm sorry, but you're just segregating yourselves." While opinions like these are often regarded as evidence of white fragility, concerns about BLM segregation also came from some of our Black participants. Tasha shared that "being Black I hear the conversations more closer and I think it is a 'us versus them.' Us versus the government. Us verses the police. Us versus all other races that think that they're mistreated." She read this perspective as "just a narrower focus on which lives matter." Ashley, too, felt "so many people, they think so close-minded . . . : 'we're sick of racism' and 'we're tired of racism' but promoting Black Lives Matter just—You know, it's stirring up more racism." In each of these responses, participants used postracialism to avoid discussing issues raised by BLM. Instead, as is common to postracial discourses, these responses projected issues of racism onto BLM's highlighting of systemic oppression.[71]

Frustrated at their inability to convince others that #ALM was preferable to BLM, many of the #ALM users we interviewed told us that neither social media nor offline discussion had offered productive space to discuss the tension between these social movements. Shelby, for example, told us her attempts to defend #ALM resulted in being "labeled that you just don't care and you don't understand and you're not listening . . . that's really not the case . . . we're just [saying] you can't solve things by separating ... and making things more divided." While Shelby hoped that sharing #ALM posts would help her "find common ground," more often she felt #ALM support would cause conflict, and "I usually try to stay out of that." Note here that Shelby's withdrawal is preemptive. Retreating into a space of predictability and stability, she uses her fear to concretize the intangible threat of conflict as BLM discourse, a concrete and thereby containable fear object. Ashley also foreclosed conversations about BLM; explaining her view that BLM is inherently racist, she told us her online response to discourses about the group was "it's time for you to get blocked because that's not what I'm trying to promote." Bob, too, had strict rules about who was allowed on his page, noting if he was "looking at your bio and we're not on the same page in some areas then I don't want to friend you. . . . 'Cause I don't want to get into a contentious argument with you." These responses represent the turn of postracialist fear seeking an object. Finding no concrete object to blame for their sense of insecurity in the world, many participants attached feelings of threat onto BLM.

The sense that BLM represented a threat to their well-being also translated into face-to-face conversations, often spilling between online and offline communication. Across our interviews, participants repeatedly framed disagreement, which ranged from direct hostility to disagreeable posts, through the lens of fear. Ahmed writes that fear is an operationalization of threat, in which we identify ourselves as either threatening or being threatened.[72] This process *causes* fear rather than grows from it. The language many of our participants used to describe their interactions with BLM supporters featured threats operationalized as BLM conflict. Steve (58, White, Locksmith) spoke often about his online and offline disagreements with his son, an avid BLM supporter. When he was speaking with his son, he told us, "I tend to avoid the subject [of BLM] because I'm just afraid that something will get said that one of us might regret, and, um, so, I kinda avoid the subject around him." By "avoid[ing] the subject," Steve removes the power from his and his son's communication behaviors, instead placing the power for division in BLM itself. In this way, Steve is able to invest his fear in BLM itself, but avoid assigning himself or his family blame for this anxiety. He effectively displaces his postracialist discomfort into BLM. Athena similarly invested her feelings of being under threat onto BLM:

> I told [my Black friends], I was like, why does it have to be just Black lives matter? I was like, that shows me right there you don't care about my well-being. You're supposed to be my friend. What if something was to happen to me? Would you rally all white lives matter? They said no.

Just as in Steve's example, Athena did not believe that her friends, supporters of BLM, were a threat, but rather that an implicit "something" might happen to her; in other words, framing herself as "under threat" as an extension of BLM discourse.[73] In these disagreements, threat is invested in the subject, BLM, rather than the individual. As a tangible object with a clear definition of ideological boundaries, BLM becomes an easy target for the investment of abstract fears.

In a postracialist culture of fear, #ALM culminates in framing BLM as a tangible object of fear. Our participants demonstrated this by arguing that BLM prevented police from protecting them from the fears they saw in the world and on social media. While Pat validated BLM's call for police reform or abolition, noting, "I have personal experience of dealing with police here in Memphis that have misused their badge," most white participants worried that racial justice rhetoric was negatively impacting their safety. Citing a rising crime rate, Brenda argued that the police are "not doing what they did in the 1980s which was proactively preventing crime. They're being reactive now because they're scared. They're scared to stop anybody, that they may be killed or have their picture taken." Diamond drew from her experience as a former police dispatcher to argue, "The police are scared of everybody." Reversing BLM's call for attention to police violence against people of color, many of our supporters believed that police were afraid of BLM. Cementing the convergence of a culture of fear and postracialist discourses, these analyses position BLM as directly preventing the police from protecting citizens. Such claims directly challenge the fact that, in Black and poor communities, police presence is itself a tangible and historically supported source of fear. Instead, these participants channeled their abstract, fragmented cultural fears into a tangible object of threat: BLM.

CONCLUSION

Just as the fear following 9/11 was channeled toward national power, allowing the United States to reinvest in military violence on behalf of fearful citizens, #ALM affiliates' abstract and dispersed fears facilitated a reinvestment in postracialism. However, unlike Ahmed's discussion of 9/11, in which "the production of the crisis . . . is crucial," #ALM required no manufactured political crisis per se.[74] Rather, posters' fears arose from all variety of locations, ranging from personal experiences with abused children to emotionally charged posts on social media. Rather than a political production of threat used to unite people through fear, the combative organization of #ALM worked in a reverse pattern; BLM organized against particular enactments of anti-Black racism, and this illustrated to those invested in postracialism that their threats were disparate and uncontained. BLM's goals aligned with the concerns of a majority of our #ALM affiliates, but their investment in colorblind ideology blocked them from the organization's communal discourse.

In this chapter, we have highlighted the ways #ALM supporters understood their own use of social media and offline discussions of the hashtag and phrase. #ALM represents the conglomeration of discourses of fear and postracialism. Just as, in chapter 3, religion and faith formed a connection between civil rights history and contemporary investments in BLM, personal experiences with fear worked to channel particular interpretations of historical threat #ALM affiliates believed were best addressed through postracialism. These personal experiences clearly illustrate the importance of individual connection to group allegiance. By tapping in to experiences of overwhelming personal affect, through experiences with bullying, child abuse, domestic violence, elder neglect, and other forms of violent behavior and imagery, messages associated with #ALM forged strong bonds with affiliates. Often this caused people who otherwise agreed with many of BLM's points to connect to #ALM instead. Though the history of civil rights organizing was admirable to many #ALM posters, they interpreted historical discussions of freedom and safety through a lens of individual experience rooted in postracialist discourse.

This chapter underscores the ambivalence underlying much contemporary culture.[75] In some ways, our results represent a disheartening trend away from community and toward private concerns. In the political context of individualism, Furedi argues, "People's response has acquired an increasingly private and personalized character. Our perception of the threat of crime is only the most tangible expression of the privatization of our fears."[76] While BLM could offer a historically rooted community for our participants, their postracial lens instead forecloses the possibility of approaching the group with open-minded understanding. In effect, these participants' fears stem from the idea that others do not share their values and principles. This fear of isolation is only exacerbated by the doubling down of individualization through resistance to social justice organizing. A productive counter-rhetoric, then, can build from the commonalities between #ALM and BLM, namely embedded fears of violence and isolation.

Indeed, #ALM posters' fears and instability also represent the increasingly public attacks on the ideological foundations of postracialism. Ono reminds us cultural politics "do not preexist rhetorical performance, and they are not sacrosanct: they are ever changing."[77] This perspective allows us to see the ways postracialism struggles to exist in a culture with increasingly public conversations surrounding race. The emergence of a culture of fear as an overt feature of postracialism may, then, signal the chipping away of such a standpoint by constant challenges from resistant discourses over the past several years.

NOTES

1. Ruth Wodak, *The Politics of Fear: What Right-Wing Populist Discourses Mean* (London: Sage, 2015).

2. Susan Smith and Rachel Pain, "Critical Geopolitics and Everyday Fears," in *Fear of Crime: Critical Voices in an Age of Anxiety*, eds. Stephen Farrall and Murray Lee (New York: Routledge, 2008), 46.

3. Brittney Cooper, "'Post-Racial America' Is a Dangerous Lie: Why the Fantasy Is Naive, Insidious and Deadly," *Salon.com*, last updated February 25, 2014, retrieved from http://www.salon.com/2014/02/25/stop_the_post_racial_fantasy_why_false_optimism_on_race_is_insidious_and_deadly/.

4. Mark Orbe, *Communication Realities in a "Post-Racial" Society: What the U.S. Public Really Thinks of President Barack Obama* (Lanham, MD: Lexington Books, 2011).

5. Kent Ono, "Postracism: A Theory of the 'Post' as Political Strategy," *Journal of Communication Inquiry* 34, no. 3 (2010): 228.

6. Ibid., 233.

7. Eduardo Bonilla-Silva, *Racism without Racists: Color-Blind Racism and Racial Inequality in Contemporary America* (Lanham, MD: Rowman & Littlefield, 2010).

8. Wodak, *The Politics of Fear*.

9. Lisa Nakamura and Peter Chow-White, *Race after the Internet* (New York: Routledge, 2012).

10. Sarah Banet-Weiser, *Authentic^{TM}: The Politics of Ambivalence in a Brand Culture* (New York: New York University Press, 2012).

11. Nakamura and Chow-White, *Race after the Internet*, 4.

12. Ibid., 3.

13. Joe R. Feagin, Hernán Vera, and Pinar Batur, *White Racism: The Basics* (New York: Routledge, 1995), 165.

14. Ono, "Postracism," 227.

15. Bonilla-Silva, *Racism without Racists*, 1.

16. Kelly Oliver, *Witnessing: Beyond Recognition* (Minneapolis: University of Minnesota Press, 2001), 164.

17. Ono, "Postracism."

18. Michael Eric Dyson, *Can You Hear Me Now?: The Inspiration, Wisdom, and Insight of Michael Eric Dyson* (New York: Basic Books, 2009).

19. Megan E. Morrissey and Christy-Dale L. Sims, "Playing the Race Card: Antiracial Bordering and Rhetorical Practices of New Racism," *The Review of Communication* 15, no. 2 (2015): 81–101; Mark Orbe, "Post-Racial Society."

20. Brittney Cooper, "Intersectionality," in *The Oxford Handbook of Feminist Theory*, eds. Lisa Disch and Mary Hakwesworth (Oxford: Oxford University Press, 2016).

21. Bonilla-Silva, *Racism without Racists*.

22. Patricia Hill Collins, *Black Sexual Politics: African Americans, Gender, and the New Racism* (New York: Routledge, 2004).

23. Ono, "Postracism," 233.

24. Cooper, "Intersectionality," 400.

25. Mark Orbe, "#AllLivesMatter as Post-Racial Rhetorical Strategy," *Journal of Contemporary Rhetoric* 5, no. 3/4 (2015); Kent Ono, "Postracism."

26. Bonilla-Silva, *Racism without Racists*.

27. Squires, Watts, Vavrus, Ono, Faye, Calafell, and Brouwer, "What Is This 'Post-.'"

28. Susan Smith and Rachel Pain, "Critical Geopolitics and Everyday Fears," in *Fear of Crime: Critical Voices in an Age of Anxiety*, eds. Stephen Farrall and Murray Lee (New York: Routledge, 2008), 46.

29. Henry A. Giroux, *The Abandoned Generation: Democracy beyond the Culture of Fear* (New York: Palgrave MacMillan, 2003).

30. Sara Ahmed, *The Cultural Politics of Emotion* (New York: Routledge, 2004).

31. Ibid., 70.

32. Ahmed, *Politics of Emotion*; Smith and Pain, *Fear of Crime*.

33. Smith and Pain, "Critical Geopolitics," 50.

34. Michael Freedan, "Editorial: Emotions, Ideology and Politics," *Journal of Political Ideologies* 18, no. 1 (2013).

35. Smith and Pain, "Critical Geopolitics."

36. Val Nicol, *Social Economies of Fear and Desire: Emotional Regulation, Emotion Management, and Embodied Autonomy* (New York: Palgrave MacMillan, 2011), 15.

37. Ahmed, *Politics of Emotion*.

38. Ibid., 70.

39. Marta Gil, "Emotions and Political Rhetoric: Perception of Danger, Group Conflict and the Biopolitics of Fear," *Human Affairs* 26, no. 2 (2016).

40. Ahmed, *Politics of Emotion*.

41. Ibid.

42. Wodak, *The Politics of Fear*.

43. Peter E. Hopkins and Susan J. Smith, "Scaling Segregation; Racializing Fear." In *Fear: Critical Geopolitics and Everyday Life*, eds. Rachel Pain and Susan J. Smith (Aldershot, Hampshire: Ashgate Publishing Limited, 2010).

44. Ibid., 72

45. Ahmed, *Politics of Emotion*.

46. Ibid.

47. Steve Goodman, *Sonic Warfare: Sound, Affect, and the Ecology of Fear* (Cambridge, MA: The MIT Press, 2010).

48. Ibid., 71.

49. Murray Lee, "The Enumeration of Anxiety: Power, Knowledge and Fear of Crime," in *Fear of Crime: Critical Voices in an Age of Anxiety*, eds. Stephen Farral and Murray Lee (New York: Routledge, 2008).

50. Ahmed, *Politics of Emotion*.

51. Marta Gil, "Emotions and Political Rhetoric."

52. Ahmed, *Politics of Emotion*, 71; Bonilla-Silva, *Racism without Racists*.

53. Nakamura and Chow-White, *Race after the Internet*, 1.

54. Heather Hensmen Kettrey and Whitney Nicole Laster, "Staking Territory in the 'World White Web': An Exploration of the Roles of Overt and Color-Blind Racism in Maintaining Racial Boundaries on a Popular Web Site," *Social Currents* 1, no. 3 (2014).

55. Gavan Titley, "No Apologies for Cross-Posting: European Trans-Media Space and the Digital Circuitries of Racism," *Crossings: Journal of Migration* 5, no. 1 (2014).

56. Marta Gil, "Emotions and Political Rhetoric."

57. Michael Freedan, "Editorial," 3.

58. Ahmed, *Politics of Emotion*, 63.

59. Ibid.

60. Ibid.

61. Ibid., 68.

62. Ibid.

63. Ibid., 68.

64. Ibid., 68.

65. Bonilla-Silva, *Racism without Racists*.

66. Oliver, *Witnessing*.

67. Ibid., 159.

68. Ono, "Postracism."

69. Bonilla-Silva, *Racism without Racists*.

70. Oliver, *Witnessing*, 164.

71. Ono, "Postracism."

72. Ahmed, *Politics of Emotion*.

73. Ibid., 72.

74. Ibid., 77.

75. Banet-Weiser, *Authentic^{TM}*.

76. Frank Furedi, *Culture of Fear Revisited* (London: Continuum, 2006), 9.

77. Ono, "Postracism," 232.

Chapter Five

"There's Nothing Else That I Can Say"

Self-Censorship in Online Racial Justice Rhetoric

In late October 2016, *The Washington Post* published an op-ed by Erika Christakis. A year previous, Christakis found herself at the center of a student and media firestorm. Following Yale's proposal to limit acceptable student Halloween costumes, including those that used racial and ethnic identities as cosplay, Christakis suggested that the policy had a laudable goal but unwisely placed free speech in the hands of university administration. The incident caught the attention of the public through a YouTube video in which students confronted Christakis, at the time a professor at the university, about her insensitivity toward marginalized students. Reflecting on this series of events in *The Post*, Christakis wrote that

> none of these examples captures the more worrying trend of self-censorship on campuses. For seven years I lived and worked on two college campuses, and a growing number of students report avoiding controversial topics—such as the limits of religious tolerance or transgender rights—for fear of uttering "unacceptable" language or otherwise stepping out of line. [1]

As was clear from the op-ed's headline, Christakis saw the incident as "a troubling lesson about self-censorship." [2] While we certainly do not mean to doubt Christakis's experiences of student self-censorship, we would add that, historically, self-censorship has been a way of life for many marginalized students with good reason to fear that sharing their experiences could make them a target of violence or ridicule. New to the twenty-first century, though, is a digital environment that allows words to travel around the globe in seconds, often with massive consequences.

In chapter 1, we argued that many contours of previous civil rights battles are present in the contemporary struggle for Black lives. The threat of state-sponsored terrorism or surveillance, which we discuss in more detail in this chapter, offers one glaring example of the ways historical legacies of racism carry into contemporary life. In Memphis, this is clearly demonstrated by the so-called Black List, an internally circulated list of eighty-four people who were to be personally escorted and surveilled any time they approached City Hall. While certainly this method of intimidation mirrors moves by city, state, and federal governments in the 1960s, this list was created in February 2017.[3] Rather than featuring names like Martin Luther King, Jr. and Malcolm X, targets of government surveillance in the mid-twentieth century, the Black List contains the names of those associated with BLM Memphis, including the mother of a teenage victim of police murder, Darius Stewart.[4] Mechanisms of surveillance were key to governmental interference in mid-twentieth-century civil rights organizing, but a key evolution in this process lies in the ease at which such information can be collected, circulated, and stored in an era of social media. As a result, conventional wisdom about protecting oneself in racial justice organizing has been updated to include a degree of self-censorship. Understanding how social media posts can harm interpersonal relationships, workplace longevity, and emotional and mental well-being, many participants in the contemporary struggle for racial justice choose to hold back ideas in the online public sphere.

In this chapter, we use the concept of self-censorship as a framework for understanding the intersection of BLM and #ALM as well as the interaction between the online self and the in-person self. This context, we argue, limits the possibilities for change, since participants perceived the interaction between the two groups, or their affiliate group and the world in general, as hostile. Understanding that online posts could have effects in their daily lives and relationships, participants often felt the need to hold back ideas and opinions. In other words, the contemporary climate of the struggle for Black lives mirrors the problems of surveillance that attempted to disrupt social justice organizing in the 1960s. In a contemporary context, these same fears, of being silenced and oppressed, were also expressed by #ALM affiliates, detracting from the ways racial justice organizing has actually threatened the livelihoods and lives of racial justice leaders historically. By examining these themes, we argue that real or perceived threats often lead to self-censorship and the consequent limiting of perspectives in racial justice conversations.

SURVEILLANCE AND THREAT IN
RACIAL JUSTICE HISTORY

Since the early days of 2012, much has been made of the silencing of various groups. Though often conservative news outlets frame the issue as discrimination at the hands of angry liberals, there is a longer and more thoroughly documented history in which oppressed groups are silenced as a way of ensuring continued political control by dominant groups. Actions by governments and citizens dedicated to maintaining status quo social structures ripple across time and weigh heavily on the minds of contemporary activists. In 1988, Public Enemy rapped about the FBI wire-tapping their phone lines, noting, "I never live alone, I never walk alone," before indicating that the assassinations of both Malcolm X and King were at the hands of the CIA.[5] This discussion, two decades after these high-profile assassinations, demonstrates the ways threats to the lives and livelihoods of civil rights activists became embedded in contemporary civil rights organizing, and the words of Public Enemy echo into BLM. Historically, threats of silence have happened through overt government threat, official surveillance, and civilian violence. Though it would take much more space to detail every incident of government or civilian threat against civil rights organizing in American history, in the space below we detail several important moments that resonate with the contemporary status of racial justice organizing in the country.

The American government has a history of threatening civil rights leaders that is as old as the country itself. One notable incident took place in the midst of World War I, at a time in which the U.S. government was deeply concerned about the possibility of "negro subversion" upsetting its military strategy overseas.[6] Writing about widespread lynching and racial terrorism in *The Crisis*, the NAACP's magazine, W. E. B. Du Bois called on readers to "battle against the forces of hell in our own land," lest African Americans demonstrate an unreciprocated loyalty to the American government.[7] Responding to the publication of this editorial, the Military Intelligence Branch of the U.S. military issued a letter to *The Crisis*'s editor, noting:

> This Branch will be glad to co-operate with you in any constructive programme which you may suggest for the eradication of any just causes for complaint, but it can not tolerate carping and bitter utterances likely to foment disaffection and destroy the morale of our people for the winning of the war.[8]

Following this clear threat by the government to silence the speech of the NAACP, Du Bois wrote an additional editorial calling for African Americans to "close ranks" with white soldiers and citizens in support of the war abroad. This editorial that would haunt Du Bois with "a mixture of shame and bitterness for the next forty years."[9] Here, the threat of censorship, particularly in the context of constant threats to Black life in the early part of the twentieth century, was enough to squelch an otherwise robust call for justice.

The government has never needed to actually threaten civil rights leaders to silence them; often official surveillance was enough to enact a chilling effect onto civil rights organizing. Begun in 1956 as the FBI Counter Intelligence Program, COINTELPRO was a massive surveillance program designed to "disrupt, discredit, and destroy the [Black Power] movement." [10] For COINTELPRO, surveillance meant more than simply wiretapping. The agency's systemic disturbance of the Black Panther Party, and groups including the Student Nonviolent Coordinating Committee among others, also involved infiltration into groups with the intention of creating mistrust, jealousy, and general dysfunction within the organization. As Lisa M. Corrigan writes, this technique had the effect of wearing down some leaders so that, absent information about COINTELPRO's real strategies, some Black Power leaders came across to the general public as paranoid and delusional. [11] Furthermore, the FBI used the agency to collect surveillance on Black liberation leaders, often deploying the resulting intelligence as a justification for imprisoning them. In this way, COINTELPRO became a government tool designed, to quote Ekwueme Michael Thelwell, "to silence and immobilize leadership while forcing groups to redirect energy and resources into raising funds, organizing legal defenses, and publicizing their cases." [12] Though CO-INTELPRO intended to work under cover of secrecy, [13] word of government interference and strategic disruption spread quickly, making clear the threat of working for Black liberation in 1960s America and beyond.

While the threat of federal government backlash certainly has a chilling effect on social movement organizing, it is not only the government who is invested in maintaining status quo anti-Black policy and culture. Public organizing for Black liberation necessarily means facing down threats of violence at the local level. Examples of violence at the hands of local and state law enforcement abound. In the spring of 1963, sit-ins and marches in downtown Birmingham were often met with high-pressure fire hoses and attack dogs. On March 7, 1965, popularly called Bloody Sunday, marchers were beaten by state troopers as they peacefully completed their protest on the Edmund Pettis Bridge. Alongside these two examples from myriad state-sponsored attacks, protesters faced violence from individuals and groups like the KKK. For example, on Mother's Day in 1961, a bus carrying the peaceful protest group the Freedom Riders was bombed, and attempts to escape the burning bus were met with white southerners who beat them with pipes, bricks, and clubs. While footage and images of these incidents may have sparked sympathy from unlikely allies, they nonetheless demonstrated the very real danger of physical violence for those who stood up for racial justice. [14]

Even amid threats of violence, loss of livelihood, and death, historical Black liberation leaders continued to push for change. Yet the memories of these attacks, generally either sponsored or ignored by the state, function as a warning for future activists and protesters. It is important that these events be documented as an integral and commonplace part of American history, but in doing so, violent backlash becomes an engrained part of any fight for justice, even and perhaps especially with the help of social media to spread ideas further and faster than ever before.

ONLINE ACTIVISM AND SELF-SURVEILLANCE

The speed at which BLM traversed the digital sphere following Mike Brown's death spoke to the salience of online communication for racial justice advocates. As Yarimar Bonilla and Jonathan Rosa write, Brown's death was documented by more than 3.6 million posts in the first week of protests in Ferguson, with over eight million posts using #Ferguson by the end of that month.[15] This barrage of posting, they argue, not only documented the protest events and information surrounding Brown's murder; it also created an avenue in which "users on Twitter felt like they were *participating in* #Ferguson."[16] This sense of communal participation has been a primary way social media has contributed to online resistance. Twitter works as a way for Black youth to interact with one another to comment on issues of identity and stereotyping in mainstream media forms.[17] Anjali Vats aligns the power of social media resistance to culture jamming, describing the conversation of Black Twitter as a way of infiltrating and undermining particular digital messages through hashtags.[18] Indeed, the Twitter platform facilitates the use of hashtags to target a particular "imagined community of users,"[19] but beyond this, as Sanjay Sharma points out, "Blacktags" have also sometimes risen to the status of trending topics on the platform, demonstrating the breadth of the resonance of racial resistance among Twitter's users.[20]

However, while expressions of identity and resistance are important sites of study, as Jessie Daniels writes, much less work has explored the ways "everyday expressions of racism" are a regular feature of online activity.[21] Like any other socially constructed place, Koen Leurs notes, "Digital spaces are not mute, neutral and external backdrops of identity formation, but distinct expressive cultures filled with ideologies, hierarchies and politics."[22] The internet was created and exists within a larger social context. Consequently, online identities and interactions do not magically rise above the white supremacist culture into which they were born. Flying in the face of early internet supporters who subscribed to the "original cyberspace promise of 'leaving the meat (body) behind,'"[23] as Lisa Nakamura and Peter Chow-White argue, online spaces have functioned to replicate and reify many of the same "complex topographies of power and privilege"[24] the digital revolution promised to alleviate. Initial ideals that understood online communication as following in the legacy of feminist and civil rights movements,[25] then, were right in that online spaces ultimately function as a space for potential revolution that is simultaneously saturated in the culture that created the oppression in the first place.

In line with the challenges of pre-digital social movements, racial justice campaigns like BLM must be understood both in terms of what is said and what is forced out of the bounds of public discourse. Heather Hensman Kettrey and Whitney Nicole Laster, for example, note that posts that appear to be written by people of color are statistically more likely to be met with explicitly racist responses than apparently white users, and users of color are often disciplined for racial discourse through appeals to colorblindness and postracialism.[26] Just as 1960s civil rights work was often met with disproportionate discursive and physical violence, Daniele Coversi's work demonstrates "quasi-spontaneous outbursts of hate speech" best described as online mobbing or cyber bullying are a regular part of the digital environment.[27] Thus we suggest a rehistoricization of Bonilla and Rosa's powerful and important claim, "It is surely not coincidental that the groups most likely to experience police brutality, to have their protests disparaged as acts of 'rioting' or 'looting,' and to be misrepresented in the media are precisely those turning to digital activism at the highest rates."[28] While we agree that the digital environment offers an affirming space of community for marginalized perspectives and identities, in much the same way as the "safe havens" of civil rights organizing in the 1960s, we question whether the numbers of visible digital activists are reduced based on the very real threats to social and physical safety posed by online condemnation of the on- and offline structures of racism.

While the digital public sphere offers a powerful tool for resistance—one that we have used for educational and activist purposes—we suggest that the literature on digital public activism and self-censorship consider the unique role of racial discipline in the censoring and obscuring of social justice discourses. Katja Rost, Lea Stahel, and Bruno S. Frey point out that online aggression, while often colloquially understood as a problem of individual self-esteem or revenge issues, is much more akin to social policing: "It accommodates a growing digital civil society that actively uses the available masses of weak ties in social media to publicly enforce social-political norms."[29] In a digital environment underscored by assumptions of postracialism, the "non-normative" discourses most likely to be disciplined are those associated with calls for racial justice.[30] While studies of online self-censorship have pointed to an abstract need for approval from others in the poster's networks,[31] this proposition does not take into account the concrete and material dangers that have been faced by marginalized communities who do not practice the ill-defined expectations set by the dominant class. In other words, the "fundamental human desires for social approval" explanation makes sense when posting photos of last night's dinner, but it stops short of explaining the very real fear of publicly rebuking White supremacy.[32]

In the following sections, we discuss the ways our participants understood the chilling effect of surveillance, even when enacted on the self, for communicating about racial justice. While the logics of self-surveillance and consequent self-censorship appeared among both BLM- and #ALM-affiliated participants, fears of workplace retribution and other material consequences were less common than in our BLM population. While BLM participants feared a loss of stability from posting an unpopular opinion, #ALM participants were more concerned with the inconvenience of online conflict. In this chapter, we focus on the self-censorship reports of our BLM participants, but include the ways this experience surfaced for #ALM affiliates at the end of the chapter.

QUIET ON THE HOME FRONT

Across both groups, self-surveillance and censorship were most commonly central to discussions of interpersonal relationships. Having discussed the issue of damage to interpersonal relationships for #ALM participants in depth in the previous chapter, here we focus on the impacts to family relationships and friendships for BLM affiliates. Participants were often aware that others in their communities might reject them over perceived disagreement on racial justice issues. In this way, participants felt disconnected from family, friends, and the culture at large.

While in-person interpersonal relationships should be mirrored online, often social media posts harmed these connections for our participants. For Len (Black, 37, Self-Employed) this issue most often arises when friends post things that conflict with her views. Expressing her apprehension about the volatility of online confrontation, she shared, she chooses not to engage. Instead, she waits for "that to be a one-on-one conversation because drama can unfold in spaces it shouldn't." While these relationships span in-person contexts and online contexts, a disconnect is often present; those who post hurtful things about Len's beliefs may not realize they are doing so, but in posting these things they are limiting the potential for interpersonal intimacy with her in their in-person relationship. Indeed, Len told us "it hurts my heart" when friends post statements denigrating BLM. Though Len once attempted to have a one-on-one conversation with a person who shared derogatory information about BLM on social media, for her, the conversation was "very surface level." She also felt that in the process, she became frustrated with her interlocutor and became the "angry Black woman," a common fear among our Black women participants. In this case, a single post created a situation that threatened Len's friendship, creating an imbalance between her and the poster.

On reflection, Len wondered how she could have done things differently. "Do I keep peace," she asked, "or do we give the lesson that day?" In this case, she chose the "peace side," reasoning that she and the person "were very close up to a certain point over the years, so I chose peace." In other words, though Len felt it was important that the person learn about the ways they had hurt her through their posts, she also realized that the conversation was not likely to change their mind. Overall, Len reported being "pretty hesitant about communicating" on BLM or #ALM. Her hesitancy grounds itself in her belief that on social media, "things get lost in translation" because the person cannot see her "nonverbals or anything like that." In sum she feels it is a waste of time going "back and forth," and she suggests that she can do something "more productive than have this virtual conversation with someone." Choosing to self-censor, then, does not preserve relationships as they had been prior to the denigrating posts, since Len had been hurt by her friend. Though it allowed the friendship to continue on the surface, the deep connection Len felt with BLM made it difficult to maintain a deep connection with her friend.

When speaking of her friends who respond to BLM with #ALM, Laura (Black, 43, Field Organizer) typically "ignores it" unless she has a "real relationship with them" and not just a "social media relationship." She says she does not want to "waste my energy or my time" or have "some type of something blow up with them and they don't know where I'm coming from." She does, however, track the person's page to see if others have "come for them" and does not think that one should "dogpile" or troll a page if someone has already made a point of disagreement. She further states

> I don't have to repeatedly beat you over the head with the same information that somebody else has obviously done a brilliant job of delivering to you, so I don't think that I should have to . . . if you read that then that's great. I don't have to compound that. I think that if it's given to you succinctly enough that you can understand it, I don't have to get in there.

In this case, Laura's behavior reflects something of a compromise between full self-censorship of participants like Len and the confrontational nature often ascribed to BLM. Rather than attempt to change someone's mind, Laura hopes for a third party to intervene, thereby educating the person for her. In this way, Laura's self-censorship is more hopeful, as she feels it will preserve her own energy without letting oppositional views go unchecked.

Self-censorship can also arise from the suspicion of trolling, or intentionally trying to upset others in an online forum. For instance, Thurmond

(Black, 55, Minister/Adjunct Professor) posted a picture he believed to be from the 1960s of a woman walking past National Guardsmen with rifles and bayonets. One of his friends asked him the meaning behind the picture. When we asked him, "Do you think they sincerely don't know or [were] they poking at you?" he responded,

> I think it's both. I think there's some people that maybe don't completely know what it means, at least one friend I have I think is being sincere when she says that. I think a couple of other people though, it's really more of a, um, maybe trying to pull me into something, or whatever. But I tend not to go . . . I will just stop. I've said what I feel, and I don't, a lot of times, I don't necessarily see the point in having prolonged debates and arguments about things, because I think going back to what you said, when people are stuck in their position and what they believe in, very often there's not a real sincere intent to maybe be open to changing it. . . . So I don't even bother with it.

Some respondents told us that self-censorship includes turning off social media notifications, actually reading and learning more about issues, or just outright blocking people from their social media pages.

Self-censorship around family and friends was not solely an online event, as many contentious conversations occurred in person as well. While the majority of our participants' immediate family were supportive, this was not universal. Kalita (White, 57, Community Activist) lamented that her husband of twenty-seven years did not "understand Black Lives Matter." When she asked him his opinion on the BLM movement, he responded that "it shouldn't be Black Lives Matter, it should be All Lives Matter." After some more discussion, she said, "That was the end of that. I didn't say anything because we have an agreement. He goes to work and I do all the social issues." Just as participants held back their ideas on social media to preserve relationships, Kalita found a way to save her marriage by self-censoring about BLM. While this is understandable, it should be noted that these relationships are in no way the same before and after the rift is discovered, since participants reported feeling hurt and sometimes personally dismissed when others were unwilling to respectfully engage with them about BLM. As we have discussed in previous chapters, the choice to engage with BLM is often sparked by the feeling that the movement connects to some part of the participants' identity. Disagreements between romantic partners, then, feel especially raw, since movement affiliation often connects to a deeper sense of self.

In an interesting contrast to Kalita's "agreement" with her husband, she told us that self-censorship in her marriage works to functionally protect her spouse's job. When speaking of her social media presence, she told us that her posts and activism in her community sometimes strokes the ire of management at her husband's place of employment. Despite her unwillingness to "put [her] family on there," she still said that her husband "gets threatened, at least once a year, that he is going to lose his job" because of her social media presence and on-the-ground activism. She said that a "vice president walks" into her husband's office at least once a year for "twenty-one years" to tell her husband that "your wife has been doing this and your, uh, we just saw your wife on the TV for that." She also notes the irony in all of this intimidation by reminding us that "he gets his job threatened, and we are white privileged!" Kalita's case was common in our discussions of self-censorship, as participants often reported feeling pressure to keep political topics to themselves.

Feeling the need to self-censor with family and friends reflected an ambivalent struggle for our participants. On one hand, affiliation with BLM or #ALM often served as an expression of some aspect of participants' identities. Feeling unable or afraid to share an aspect of their identity, particularly one that was being discussed so frequently in-person or on social media, was painful for many. On the other hand, because they recognized how deeply these affiliations ran, participants were keenly aware of the relational damage that could be done through a conflict over BLM and #ALM. Thus, participants often expressed being caught in a dilemma, realizing that whether or not they chose to confront those in their family and friend groups about disagreements, once these conflicts were revealed, the relationship would likely never be the same.

THE ECONOMIC THREAT OF RESISTANCE

While the threat of losing friends and family was very real for our participants, a more harrowing consequence comes in the threat of losing one's livelihood. Here, participants often felt divided between sharing with others and protecting themselves, realizing that the workplace offered both a space for persuasion and a potentially hostile environment. Chanel (Black, 28, Nonprofit Program Coordinator) told us that her co-workers sometimes approached her to discuss current events related to police violence against Black women and men: "Being one of two African Americans on our very small staff, it has [been] brought up . . . [I'll talk to] anybody willing to have a conversation because it's just something that I'm really passionate about . . . " While Chanel did not self-censor, she did note that conversations at work had to be cautious. She clarified that "not everybody [at work] is ready to deal with [discussions about BLM] . . . it's very hush hush." Though Chanel was clear in telling us that these discussions most often came up when white co-workers engaged her in conversation about current events, she described her vigilance in keeping the conversation calm and reserved.

Other participants, though, noted that they preferred to avoid topics like BLM altogether. Peralto (Black, 34, Pharmacy Tech) vacillated in his discussion of professional self-censorship: "I talk at work but, end up. . . . Well, I don't talk at work, partly because of me," he laughed. After interjecting that he had "de-friended everybody at work," Peralto told us he suggests his co-workers look at his public social media pages if they are curious about his views on BLM. As he shared, "I tell them, if you go to my page and look, you can see what you want . . . but that means you went there to see, and I'm not hiding anything from you." Peralto's responses demonstrate an ambivalence about professional self-censorship. On one hand, he does not want to communicate with his co-workers about BLM, but on the other, he does not see himself hiding his views. While he is not connected with co-workers on social media, he directs them to his pages. In this way, in-person self-censorship clearly intersects with online racial justice communication, where controversial views can be shielded from the workplace by directing co-workers to an online presence.

Peralto's realization of the consequences of disagreement battled with his passion for spreading information about BLM. This tension, between participants' passionate views on BLM and their need to maintain a more neutral image in the workplace, speaks to the emotional connections participants felt with the movement. Neese (Black, 37, Clerk) explained that she tries to appear "nice on Facebook," largely because she knows her emotional attachments to discussions on social media will spill over into her daily life. As she noted, "I'm emotionally involved, so I try to not even be heated because imma be heated at work and I can't even get to that person and say, 'You stupid.' (laughing) So I shy away from it on Facebook." Because Neese sought to remain professional at work, she censored her behavior on social media as it relates to BLM and other political views, but this did not stop her from feeling intensely invested in the movement.

The sense that emotional investment in the BLM movement opened participants up for the threat of workplace punishment often arose as an extension of working in a predominantly white workplace. Neese remembered this from the 2008 election, when "if you worked with anyone white, you could hear a pin drop. No one wanted to discuss the election." Asking rhetorically and, it seemed, sarcastically, she questioned, "Why? Why? What, what difference is it? Color makes a difference?" This avoidance of discussing issues of race carried over to BLM in the contemporary workplace, as Ganda (African American, 35, Student/Research Assistant) told us: "I work . . . in an environment where I'm the only Black person. So when we go to meetings, anything, I'm the only Black person in a lot of faces . . . so a lot of my co-workers and my employers are my friends on social media and everything, so I feel like I have to limit and kind of always filter what I really . . . feel." Though Ganda's social media presence was separate from her professional demeanor, she understood that these spheres are connected, so she used self-censorship on her private social media pages to protect her career. The ability to openly invest in BLM, then, was not only limited to traditionally public or private sphere communications, then, since the two are intertwined through social media.

Professional self-censorship, particularly as it relates to BLM, worked directly in conversation with the types of racial injustices BLM seeks to address. In particular, participants noted that their fears often stemmed from the over-representation of white women and men in management roles. Peralto described this role of professional standards in self-censorship behaviors as historical. He explained that the civil rights movement helped many Black men and women to "[get] a job, you had to go to work, and then your capacity to affect change was limited to, at that point." In describing the trajectory of social movements alongside that of Black career advancement, Peralto pointed to the silencing of Black protest in the name of respectability. The awareness that white people could always be watching their behavior and that these people controlled hiring and firing decisions impacted online and offline communication about BLM. Blair (African American, 21, Student) explained.

> Blair: I wrestle between should I be very vocal or should I control what I say. And I say that because I'm going to need white people to hire me, because that's who, that's who are in charge of, you know, the jobs and careers that I want to aspire to . . . I fall into this respectability politics order, but it's so hard, it's mentally exhausting and it's really hard.

> Dan (Persian/Caucasian, 24, Student): It's spiritually demeaning.

> Blair: I can't really, I can't be myself. It's like I have to choose to talk so proper to someone.

Respectability, here, applied both to style and manner of speaking and to more specific censoring practices involved with speaking out on social movements. In this way, code switching was not limited to just the presentation of ideas, but to the ideas themselves. The perception of a workplace, school, or culture as white dominated, then, resulted in the suppression of self in individuals. Since BLM affiliation reflected a connection to individual identity, particularly in terms of racial identification, the historical precedent that threatens movement participation at work also inhibited participants' ability to discuss race with co-workers.

The fear that social media commentary on racial issues would carry over into employment opportunities was confirmed by Ganda, who recalled, "I worked for a city for eleven years, and I worked in a position where those are the things we checked. We found your social media account. . . . For my people, it's 'Oh, yea, she's proud. She's aware. It's conscious' . . . but for white people? Like I said, I'm like the angry Black woman." Speaking of the threat of losing professional and personal accomplishments, Ganda described a "fear of things being taken from you, so let me hold it as tight as I can to me":

Ganda: I have to almost always kind of think about [what I tweet] . . . sometimes I'll be going, going, going, and get ready to hit that post button and something will just stop me and say—

Ivory (Black, 23, Student/Sales Associate): Hold on.

Ganda: think about what you—because these are the things that people use against you. Especially the one little Black girl that's so damn angry.

. . .

Ganda: I'm almost not biting my tongue, because I don't bite my tongue when I type, but that's what I have to do is hold my fingers, because that social media can be deadly.

Ivory: You don't want it to be used against you . . . that's another form of oppression.

Many of our women participants echoed the fear that the "angry Black women" stereotype would be used against them as evidence of their unprofessionalism. Speaking of a university class setting, Blair told us one of her white professors subordinated BLM to #ALM, a claim that she found deeply offensive. Despite her strong emotional reaction to this statement, she "couldn't even say anything because I'm one of two Black girls in the class and every time I say something I get this stigma that I'm the angry Black woman." The felt necessity for self-censorship at work and school, then, not only demanded the suppression of movement affiliation, but also the constant self-surveillance of racial identity. Movement identification was so closely tied to racial identity in many cases that these were not separate, but deeply interwoven, ideas.

The intertwining identities of participants' race and movement identity, and the idea that these connected selves must be constantly monitored and tempered, worked together to limit the ways participants discussed BLM. Extending beyond the "angry Black woman" stereotype, many men in our groups similarly felt they would be accused of emotional excess if they discussed their affiliation with BLM. When we asked whether participants would be concerned about discussing BLM and other issues of racial justice at work, Peralto told us he worried about

> becoming the guy—that guy. You know the troublemaker. I mean, they already refer to me as the angry Black man. (laughing) That's my nick-name. . . . But you can't [feel like] I'm harassing you with my views.

> RBG (Black, 45, Sales): Tell the truth, you're angry.

> Peralto: Angry Black man. Yea. So the workplace gotta be interesting for a lot of us.

> [General consensus crosstalk from the group]

> RBG: I tiptoe on the line sometimes at work too.

In fact, participants saw this as a form of making an example of someone, mirroring practices of public lynchings and assassinations in the Jim Crow South and during the civil rights movement. As Kalita explained, "Here in the South . . . a lot of messages are sent or conveyed about a person or a message and it's not just to kill the messenger, but to show the community that if you do this too, we're going to do this to you." April agreed with this assessment, calling the tactic "fear and intimidation," to which Kalita responded, "So, if you don't want that to happen to you, you better not do what she's doing or write what she's writing or say what she's saying."

SELF-CENSORSHIP FOR SELF-CARE

While much of the literature exploring the fight for Black liberation over the generations has focused on the battle between movements and external threats of violence, equally important is the issue of sustaining energy for long-term struggle. Recently, online activists and sympathizers have revived Audre Lorde's assertion that "caring for myself is not self-indulgence, it is self-preservation, and that is an act of political warfare" by sharing it widely in social media posts and think pieces.[33] Not only is online disagreement and debate an exhausting and laborious process, often with very little reward, in the case of Black BLM participants, online argument is commonly a debate over their value as human beings. The fatigue at having to argue with some-one about whether or not you should be able to assert that your life matters, coupled with the very real historical threat of state-sanctioned surveillance and punishment, means that many of our participants choose to self-censor as a way of maintaining their emotional well-being.

Often, Black BLM supporters expressed frustration at being asked to defend their own value in the eyes of those who did not seem to see them as multi-dimensional human beings. Ganda, for example, told us that one of the most frustrating things for her on social media is to correct what she feels are stereotypes demeaning Black people—especially Black women. For Ganda, this set up a dualism in her online identity. On one hand, in resisting the "angry Black woman" trope, she shared that she typically does not "bite her tongue" when expressing herself. In her daily interactions, she is open to discussing her frustrations with others, particularly in the area of race. On the other hand, she felt social media was a much more threatening place to share. This inner conflict left her feeling as though "I have to bite my tongue. I feel like I don't get the full. I definitely feel sometimes like—you know, why can't I just put what I really want to put." While Ganda's identity crosses over between in-person and online interactions, the social media atmosphere and its threat of surveillance and retaliation leads her to hold back her opinions. In other words, while her identity is constant across real life and online platforms, her behavior reflects a deep awareness of the dangers associated with standing up for her value as a human.

Self-censorship as a mode of self-care also carries over in classrooms. Blair shared a story with us about a professor of hers saying that BLM "stems from All Lives Matter." While she felt compelled to challenge or question the professor's assertion, she felt she could not say anything because as "one of the two Black girls in the class . . . every time I say something I get this stigma that I'm the angry Black woman when I'm being so passionate about . . . what we talk about." Like Ganda, Blair's self-censorship was an act of resistance both to the emotional demands of educating others and to the exhausting effects of managing one's identity in the face of persistent stereotypes. To stand up for her beliefs would be, for some in the room, to perform the stereotype used to silence her in the first place. In other words, by asserting that they are more than a stereotype, Black women like Blair are perceived as actually performing the stereotype. Attempts to navigate her beliefs and her identity in the classroom and elsewhere meant that she had "gotten to a point now I'm tired of convincing white people that we deserve equality. If you can't see that for yourself, I'm done. . . . It's not my job to convince you that I deserve to be treated equally." That Blair cared deeply about Black liberation but chose to self-censor for her own self-care is not a contradiction, but a consistency. As with many of our participants, the attachment to BLM came from a deeply felt connection between the movement and salient aspects of identity performance. Care for her own human dignity and self-determination as a Black woman, then, caused both her investment in BLM and her decision to refrain from fighting with white people about her right to that same dignity and determination. Self-censorship for self-care reflects the same investment in a part of one's identity that caused participants to engage in the first place.

The twin investment in self-censorship and identity becomes all the more tragic when understood in the context of threats to movement leaders and participants, something that looms particularly close in Memphis. Not only does the city have a deep history of engagement in social movements, but it was also the location of King's assassination in 1968. Springing from this history, the realization that self-censorship was both necessary and wise arose across the board in our interviews. Kalita expressed the wisdom of self-censorship as a mode of self-care. While supporting and advocating online for BLM, she told us she would not feel safe wearing a BLM shirt in her community and around her friends. She shared with us a time where she thought about getting a BLM shirt, but began to wonder, "Where would I wear that shirt? How would I wear that shirt?" Calling the shirt "provocative," she decided against purchasing it because of safety concerns in her home just south of Memphis:

> Now that people can carry guns in Mississippi, even into churches . . . I decided I would not wear that on my body because I cannot control the racist, the, the racist white men that I live with in Mississippi. And I cannot control myself that I would be subservient or say something they did not want to hear. So to me wearing that shirt in Mississippi would be trouble, so I didn't get it.

As her comment makes clear, Kalita's fear here was of violence, a very real material threat. Yet often the conversation about material threats centers on asserting the reality of violence in communities of color, obfuscating the ways the threat itself can lead to fatigue and worry. In this case, Kalita felt wearing the shirt may spark a confrontation, and that she would feel she needed to "answer to it." This conversation foregrounds the energy Kalita spent thinking through the possible outcomes of something as simple as purchasing a T-shirt in support of a cause that was important to her. In this case, to simply refrain from purchasing, then wearing, the T-shirt worked as both an act of self-censorship and an act of self-care. By refusing to purchase the shirt, and self-censoring in the process, she allowed herself to let go of the worry of attack that accompanied her consideration of the purchase. Investment in self-care, again, was a simultaneous investment in the memory of social movement history.

Each of these cases speaks to the ways threats of retribution, abundant in the history of Black liberation movements, creates stress and exhaustion in those who continue the fight in the BLM era. As a result, and on the advice of movement figure Audre Lorde, many of our participants were careful about their speech. In self-censoring, these participants cared for their own emotional and mental needs, putting themselves first for a moment. In doing so,

Lorde reminds us, these movement members preserve their energy and health for later fights. While this form of self-censorship reflects a re-investment in BLM that is oppositional to its appearance of retreat, it remains deeply unfair that they are made to feel silenced in communicating their own value as humans.

#ALM AND THE RESISTANCE TO CONFLICT

The idea of self-censorship for self-care was not exclusive to BLM affiliates. Across the board, participants described social media disagreement as an energy drain. This is notable, since history tells us that #ALM participants had little reason to worry that their posts could cause material loss, state-sanctioned violence, or ongoing surveillance. Yet the act of arguing online was fatiguing enough to result in self-censorship in many cases. Because these participants were as invested in the connection they felt between #ALM and their identities, engaging those who denied its role seemed insurmountable.

Though it manifested differently for BLM participants than for #ALM participants, the idea of avoiding conversations because they are generally unpleasant was common across the board. While BLM participants often referenced overt danger in discussing self-censorship as self-care, #ALM participants wanted to maintain either their online identity or their energy. First, concerned with her online identity, Brenda (White, 67, Retired Business Owner) told us she worried about things she saw on Facebook that conflicted with her Christian faith. Describing posts from social media connections who identify as Atheists, Brenda told us, "Some of their posts can be very offensive to me because I, I am a Christian . . . I don't want people to see that on my timeline." To clarify, Brenda was concerned that if she commented or interacted with the post, it would appear on her friends' timelines with her name attached, something that is plausible if the post was public. Brenda therefore refrained from commenting on things she disagreed with but told us "I won't unfriend them because I want them to see my posts that I share that . . . it may, it may change their mind." Brenda intentionally avoided engaging with these friends for fear of impacts on her online identity; while she was not open to ideas that challenged her ideological investments, she hoped others might be persuadable.

Like Brenda, Bob (White, 50, Sales) was not interested in having oppositional ideas appear on his timeline. Before he accepted any follow request, he told us, he vetted the requester to be sure they were primarily in agreement on social issues:

> You got to be discerning on who you follow and who follows you . . . you can disagree with me, I don't want you following 'cause I'm not gonna have an

argument. I don't want you filling my pages up with droop, kay? "Well they
have free speech." Well free speech starts somewhere else, okay? Go somewhere else. I don't want to hear you. The same as somebody's at the corner
yelling something crazy. I can either go stand there and listen to him, or I can
drive on. Well I choose to drive on.

Bob's concern that those who disagree with him would result in his pro-
file "filling . . . up with droop" speaks to the idea of maintaining a stream-
lined personal identity online. Affiliating with #ALM demonstrates an investment with a particular aspect of the participant's identity, and by affiliating publicly, group members often hoped to build and reinforce their communities. This meant that they were engaged in protecting that identity connection and ensuring that it remained pure, both for themselves and for others
who might encounter their social media presence. Speaking about the racism
she felt BLM brought to most conversations, Ashley (Black, 26, Waitress)
told us BLM affiliates were "getting on here and you're starting a, a comment war with hate and bashing towards another person who you do not
know, you know? And if that isn't racism, I just don't know what is. So,
yeah, it's time for you to get blocked because that's not what I'm trying to
promote." Ashley's reference to "promot[ing]" a perceived attack speaks to
the role many of our participants felt social media could play in conflict. For
Ashley, blocking people she perceived to be uncivil protected her identity by
keeping it pure from the influences of BLM. She did not want her name
affiliated with BLM, even in cases of disagreement, lest her conflict serve to
unintentionally promote the views of her opposition.

Like Brenda and Ashley, Bob was concerned about his identity online,
but Bob's comment also speaks to a second area of concern for many posters:
the maintenance of energy. As he went on to explain, "If you're not mutual
friends or I'm looking at your bio and we're not on the same page in some
areas then I don't want to friend you . . . I don't want to get into a contentious
argument with you." #ALM Participants often took on an air of exhaustion
when describing their decisions to self-censor. Though Shelby (White, 52,
Physical Therapist) was interested in "trying to strike a conversation about,
you know, maybe trying to find a way to have some common ground," she
was also largely disinterested in engaging with those who disagreed with her
views. Like other participants from both groups, both BLM and #ALM,
Shelby sensed that conversations across the aisle were predominantly fruit-
less. As she told us, "Sometimes it's, it's an agreement, and other times it's,
you know, [a controversy]. I usually try to stay out of that." Though Shelby
did not express fear that participating in conflicts online could harm her
reputation, she saw contentious arguments as unproductive and therefore
chose to refrain from participation.

Whereas our #ALM participants often framed self-censorship as an issue of avoiding conflict, a few of our #ALM participants expressed the idea that picking fights with others could be enjoyable. Steve (White, 58, Locksmith), for example, described responding to posts on his son's social media pages, noting, "I can put my two cents in. I do this just for fun sometimes, and his friends will jump all over me like fleas on a dog. Uh, it's just, you know, they're so young, they're so energetic in their opinion and not yet . . . too tired to fight for stupid, extreme little things." Steve's description of provoking others was not common, but it offers an important insight into the ways public debate often plays out online; a debate between a person who justly understands BLM as a fight for their own life and a person who sees the debate as sport is unlikely to be balanced or fair. In the 1960s, the state strategy of fomenting discord within civil rights organizations unbalanced and distracted the real work of racial justice. Today, some of this work has transferred to the private citizen who views debates over the value of Black lives as entertainment. Though uncommon among our #ALM participants, a primary threat of #ALM lies in the members who aim to stir things up, keep people on edge, and maintain constant the threat of disagreement, historically manifested in violence and threats to life and livelihood.

CONCLUSION

Following the tradition of government and civilian actions that threaten those who speak up for justice, social media often encourages self-censorship. BLM advocates understand the threat to their interpersonal relationships, both online and off, as well as the ways some employers view anti-racist programs as controversial. Understandably, then, many of our participants reported keeping ideas to themselves in attempt to protect themselves from retribution. Holding back these ideas, though, carries its own risks, since participants' sense of well-being was often threatened by internal conflicts about whether or not they should participate in online and in-person discussions. In many cases, the decision to hold back ideas was as much about preserving their own sense of spiritual calm as it was about fearing overt or material backlash. As such, we argued in this chapter that online communication offers a new challenge for social justice organizing, even as it facilitates more widespread message circulation. Taking the place of overt surveillance and disruption mechanisms, such as COINTELPRO, the knowledge that things said online can have real impacts in our material lives held individuals back from fully participating in social media discussions.

At the same time, organized state-sponsored surveillance and counter-activism programs persist alongside this new mechanism of online self-censorship. In Memphis, the Black List emerged as a way of tracking those who struggle for justice against police violence, with similar programs targeting activists and participants at the state and federal level. It should come as no surprise, then, that many who might participate in or support BLM are persuaded otherwise through the threat of backlash. When faced with the threat of losing relationships, jobs, and a general sense of calm and well-being, it is understandable that many on the side of resistance would keep silent. Yet their silence does not reflect a disengagement from or lack of investment in BLM or #ALM. These movements were deeply rooted in a sense of connection with participants' identities, so that refraining from advocacy actually reflected a more intense investment in BLM or #ALM; for many of our participants, the close association between the movement and their identities called for protection, even when that protection meant self-surveillance and self-censorship.

In previous chapters we have argued that affiliation with BLM and #ALM reflected participants' connection to political history filtered through a lens of individual, everyday experience. Unfortunately, this pattern is as true for lack of engagement as it is for engagement. Instances of self-censorship reflect movement affiliates' awareness of historical trends of suppressed speech filtered through their own experience with censure. Connection to BLM and #ALM are deeply personal, a trait that makes behaviors and ideas within the movement and countermovement difficult to predict. Yet as explanations for self-censorship demonstrate, always predictable is the impact of precedent, in which individuals learn to predict responses and backlash and act, or not act, accordingly.

NOTES

1. Erika Chistakis, "My Halloween Email Led to a Campus Firestorm—and a Troubling Lesson about Self-Censorship," *Washington Post*, October 28, 2016, https://www.washingtonpost.com/opinions/my-halloween-email-led-to-a-campus-firestorm--and-a-troubling-lesson-about-self-censorship/2016/10/28/70e55732-9b97-11e6-a0ed-ab0774c1eaa5_story.html?utm_term=.e9088b7cc6b1.

2. Ibid.

3. WMC Action News 5 Staff, "City Hall Releases Updated 'Blacklist,'" *WMC Action News 5*, March 1, 2017, http://www.wmcactionnews5.com/story/34638607/names-added-to-city-hall-Blacklist-in-error-have-been-removed.

4. Ibid.

5. Public Enemy, "Louder Than a Bomb," June 28, 1988, Chung King Studios and Greene St. Recording in Manhattan, Sabella Studios in Long Island, Track 7, *It Takes a Nation of Millions to Hold Us Back*, 1988, cassette.

6. "Calls for Racial Justice Silenced 1917," David M. Rubenstein Gallery, National Archives, retrieved from http://recordsofrights.org/events/70/calls-for-racial-justice-silenced.

7. Qtd. in Wray R. Johnson, "Black American Radicalism and the First World War: The Secret Files of the Military Intelligence Division," *Armed Forces and Society* 26, no. 1 (1999).

8. Letter archived online at "The Loyalty of the American Negro" 1917, David M. Rubenstein Gallery, National Archives, retrieved from http://recordsofrights.org/records/189/the-loyalty-of-the-american-negro/1.

9. Mark Ellis, "'Closing Ranks' and 'Seeking Honors': W. E. B. Du Bois in World War I," *The Journal of American History* 79, no. 1 (1992): 96.

10. Lisa M. Corrigan, *Prison Power* (Jackson: University of Mississippi Press, 2017), 13.

11. Ibid.

12. Ekwueme Michael Thelwell, "Foreword," *Die Nigger Die!* (Chicago, IL: Lawrence Hill, 1969), xxi–xxii.

13. Kristen Hoerl and Erin Ortiz, "Organizational Secrecy and the FBI's COINTEL-PRO–Black Nationalist Hate Groups Program, 1967–1971," *Management Communication Quarterly*, 29 (2015): 590–615.

14. Victoria J. Gallagher and Kenneth S. Zagacki, "Visibility and Rhetoric: Epiphanies and Transformations in the Life Photographs of the Selma Marches of 1965," *Rhetoric Society Quarterly* 37, no. 2 (2007): 113–35.

15. Yarimar Bonilla and Jonathan Rosa, "#Ferguson: Digital Protest, Hashtag Ethnography, and the Racial Politics of Social Media in the United States," *American Ethnologist* 42, no. 1 (2015): 4–17.

16. Ibid., p. 7, emphasis original.

17. Jodi L. Rightler-McDaniels and Elizabeth M. Hendrickson, "Hoes and Hashtags: Constructions of Gender and Race in Trending Topics," *Social Semiotics* 24, no. 2 (2014): 175–90.

18. Anjali Vats, "Cooking Up Hashtag Activism: #PaulasBestDishes and Counternarratives of Southern Food," *Communication and Critical/Cultural Studies* 12, no. 2 (2015): 209–13.

19. Axel Bruns and Jean Burgess, "The Use of Twitter Hashtags in the Formation of Ad Hoc Publics," Paper presented at the European Consortium for Political Research conference, Reykjavik (August 25–27, 2011), 804.

20. Sanjay Sharma, "Black Twitter? Racial Hashtags, Networks and Contagion," *New Formation* 78 (2013): 51.

21. Jessie Daniels, "Race and Racism in Internet Studies: A Review and Critique," *New Media and Society* 15, no. 5 (2012): 710.

22. Koen Leurs, "Digital Passages: Moroccan-Dutch Youths Performing Diaspora, Gender and Youth Cultural Identities across Digital Space" (PhD diss., Utrecht University, 2012), 22.

23. Sharma, "Black Twitter?" 46.

24. Lisa Nakamura and Peter A. Chow-White, "Introduction—Race and Digital Technology: Code, the Color Line, and the Information Society," in *Race after the Internet*, ed. Lisa Nakamura and Peter A. Chow-White (New York: Routledge, 2012), 17.

25. Lisa Nakamura, *Digitizing Race: Visual Culture of the Internet* (Minneapolis: University of Minnesota Press, 2008).

26. Heather Hensman Kettrey and Whitney Nicole Laster, "Staking Territory in the 'World White Web': An Exploration of the Roles of Overt and Color-Blind Racism in Maintaining Racial Boundaries on a Popular Web Site," *Social Currents* 1, no. 3 (2014): 257–74.

27. Daniele Conversi, "Irresponsible Radicalization: Diasporas, Globalization and Long-Distance Nationalism in the Digital Age," *Journal of Ethnic and Migration Studies* 38, no. 9 (2012): 1371.

28. Bonilla and Rosa, "#Ferguson," 8.

29. Katja Rost, Lea Stahel, and Bruno S. Frey, "Digital Social Norm Enforcement: Online Firestorms in Social Media," *PLoS One* 11, no. 6 (2016): 17.

30. Conversi, "Irresponsible Radicalization."

31. K. Hazel Kwon, Shin-Il Moon, and Michael A. Stefanone, "Unspeaking on Facebook? Testing Network Effects on Self-Censorship of Political Expressions in Social Network Sites," *Quality and Quantity* 49, no. 4 (2016); Steven Reiss, "Multifaceted Nature of Intrinsic Motivation: The Theory of 16 Basic Desires," *Review of General Psychology* 8 (2004).

32. Kwon, Moon, and Stefanon, "Unspeaking on Facebook?"

33. See for example, "Selfcare as Warfare," *Feminist Killjoys*, August 25, 2014, https://feministkilljoys.com/2014/08/25/selfcare-as-warfare/; Sarah Mirk, "Audre Lorde Thought of Self-Care as an 'Act of Political Warfare,'" *Bitch Media*, February 18, 2016, https://www.bitchmedia.org/article/audre-lorde-thought-self-care-act-political-warfare; Krystal Reddick, "Self-Care as Revolutionary Action," *Huffington Post*, January 6, 2015, https://www.huffingtonpost.com/krystal-reddick/selfcare-as-revolutionary_b_6393154.html.

Conclusion

From Margins to Center

We began this book by tracing the deeply felt tragedy of Trayvon Martin's murder, followed two and a half years later by Michael Brown's murder. While these two unjust deaths mark moments of traction for BLM, they are in no way isolated. BLM has worked as a lens, documenting the murders of Eric Garner, Tamir Rice, Sandra Bland, Freddie Gray, Alton Sterling, Korryn Gaines, Jordan Edwards, Charleena Lyles, and too many others. Indeed, in the week between drafting this conclusion and revising it, Stephon Clark was shot eight times in the back by police in his grandmother's back yard,[1] and officials announced that the police officer who killed Alton Sterling will not face criminal charges.[2] By circulating news of these murders, BLM has mapped the systemic nature of police violence, and anti-Black violence more generally. BLM affiliates in Memphis, too, have mapped the ways these incidents of violence are linked to other structural issues including education, housing, nutrition, clean water, political representation, and surveillance, among others. In a context of postracialism, BLM has succeeded in highlighting not only the fact that anti-Black racism remains a problem, but *how* that problem manifests. Part of this documentation includes scrutiny of how the simple call for Black lives to matter culturally, economically, politically, and otherwise resulted in the fierce backlash marked by hashtags like #WhiteLivesMatter, #PoliceLivesMatter, #BlueLivesMatter, and of course #ALM.

Yet despite the clear context of anti-Black racism into which #ALM emerged, this hashtag, too, is more complex than it seems on its surface. Less traceable and often less concrete than the structural concerns of BLM affiliates, the fears and insecurities of #ALM posters emerge not only and not always as a disparagement of BLM. The ways BLM and #ALM converge, parallel, and split again speak to the complexity of motivation in a cultural

111

context marked by histories of social organizing and fragmentation in an era divided and networked by social media. This book, therefore, has been a documentation of the ways BLM and #ALM unfolded in the greater Memphis area. In particular, we were interested not only in documenting the cultural contexts that drive social movements, but also in understanding the motivations of those who actively spread those discourses. In other words, we wanted to understand these social movements from a perspective not readily available through the rhetorical analysis of speeches or other public texts, but from a lens that considered individual movement affiliates and how they understand their role in social (in)justice.

With that in mind, we structured this book to account for the various contexts that emerged in our discussions with participants. First, we argued that historical context grounded much of BLM's meanings, as BLM participants both echoed sentiments of mid-twentieth-century civil rights leaders and distanced themselves from those structures. This historical context, of course, applies to structures of white supremacy, which we then turned to in chapter 2. Here, we noted the complexities of racial conversation, both applying and stretching the well-travelled concept of white fragility. Chapter 3 took up Christianity's relationship with BLM, marking the ways religion motivated and contextualized participants' sense of connection with the movement and one another. In chapter 4, we discussed the function of the culture of fear combined with a context of postracialism. Here, we argued that fear was a primary motivating factor in drawing participants into #ALM, as the countermovement sometimes appeared as a space for exorcising frustrations that were less structurally organized than those prioritized by BLM. Considering the larger economies of work and family, we then turned to the motivations for sharing or, more saliently, for not sharing. Finally, in chapter 5, we examined the ways threats of surveillance and discipline function as a context for sharing information on BLM. While our BLM-affiliated participants all shared information on the movement through both social media and interpersonal channels, this sharing was marked by moments of fear and self-censorship informed by real threats to job security and cultural capital. Though fear was common to BLM and #ALM participants, this context of threat worked differently for #ALM-affiliated participants. Throughout these chapters, we have explored the various angles important to our participants, using their words to structure our arguments. In so doing, we have centered the ways participants understand both BLM and #ALM as online and offline phenomena, contributing a new vernacular perspective to the scholarship on BLM and social movements generally.

Across these thematically organized chapters, history is a constant. As audience-studies scholars have long argued, the meaning of media does not simply rest in the text but is formed at the moment when a text meets its audience.[3] For BLM and #ALM affiliates, that moment of meaning was framed by national and individual histories. Contemporary social movements are often studied through a lens of national histories. Movement leaders are compared to historical movement leaders and demonstrations to previous demonstrations. This was clear for our participants, who often discussed being directly motivated by their understandings of historical social movements. Remembering the words of Malcolm X and Martin Luther King, Jr., for example, allowed movement participants to make sense of BLM and understand its potential as a force for change.

However, most misunderstandings of BLM and #ALM stemmed from the misremembering of history. The idea that BLM was "not your grandparents' movement," for example, highlights the ways civil rights organizing has been systematically misremembered. Discussions of Martin Luther King, Jr.'s ideas often rob them of their radical nature, forgetting that the FBI had labeled the leader "the most dangerous Negro in America."[4] Forgetting King's radicalism distances current BLM affiliates from the hard-won lessons of past civil rights organizing. It also provides fodder for #ALM affiliates who argue BLM is dangerously radical. This last point is crucial, because the perception that BLM was radically different from the Civil Rights movement prevented many from supporting the movement that best aligned with their political positions. Many of the #ALM affiliates we spoke with were not so oppositional to BLM as to be unpersuadable. Rather, many #ALM posters shared all or most of BLM's values. Again, it is a misremembered history that positions social and countermovements as oppositional, rather than realizing that these discourses happen along a spectrum. This misremembering has the effect of encouraging dichotomous thinking in the present and future. While certainly some #ALM posters were never going to be persuaded to join BLM, imagining all #ALM affiliates as a white supremacist monolith functioned to divide potential allies rather than encourage coalitional politics. A more nuanced understanding of history would serve contemporary social movements well, both accurately honoring the contributions of former movement organizers and more realistically mapping social dynamics during times of cultural tension and change.

One aspect of understanding the nuance of history for BLM and #ALM affiliates is to consider national history in conversation with personal history. As we have argued in this book, those who join movements do so because they see a connection between the movement and some aspect of their own lives. Sometimes these connections fit cultural assumptions. Many of our Black BLM participants referenced hearing stories of anti-Black violence from parents and grandparents, making clear the connection between their lived experiences and BLM's platform. However, 59 percent of the #ALM affiliates we interviewed were Black, so family experiences with anti-Black violence is not, alone, a predictor of movement affiliation. This not only points to the inaccuracy of imaging African Americans as a political monolith, but also to the difficulty in predicting allegiances based on racial and other demographics. Rather, participation is motivated by the perception that individual histories are addressed by a movement's platform.

Movements are strongest when their platform is straightforward and concrete, as with BLM's "Vision for Black Lives."[5] We are not suggesting that movement platforms should address every problem. Rather, in conversation with this book's focus on the connection between online and offline movement participation, we interpret the individualized nature of motivation as a call for communication. While it would be difficult for "the movement" as an abstract entity to communicate the ways the platform reaches all possible people, it behooves supporters to seek out potential members and find ways of connecting the movement's message to individual histories of trauma and joy. In many cases, as with #ALM participants concerned with education, crime, and poverty, BLM's platform offered an organized way of targeting their primary concerns. The difficulty was often a hesitation about whether BLM was exclusive or inclusive, a confusion driven by the misremembering and misunderstanding of the ways social movements work and have worked historically. By reframing movement platforms to speak to individualized experiences, participants can recruit others into mutually beneficial coalitions. Given the individual specificity of participants' concerns, this is an issue not of platform, but of the messy unpredictability of people.

A MOVEMENT IS ITS PEOPLE

The historical foundation for online and offline movement participation is crucial to moving forward with contemporary social change organizing, but it is complicated by the messiness of human interaction. Consequently, we approached our analysis of BLM and #ALM through a lens of individual participants' perspectives. In doing so, we have attempted to highlight several implications that we believe should be central to the future of social movement rhetoric in practice and scholarship.

First, rhetorical and media scholars are uniquely positioned to document social movement rhetoric in real time, as movements arise and unfold. Though we realize our application of audience ethnography or participatory critical rhetoric is perhaps a departure from what Martin J. Medhurst imagined when he called on public address scholars to take up the "historical preservation of rhetorical materials and artifacts," we understand this project as an extension of his call.[6] Asking scholars of traditional public address "to think like anthropologists and curators," Medhurst pointed out artifacts lost to history are forever lost from study as well.[7] In a field dependent upon texts, we must preserve those texts. While the age of the Internet aids us in documenting social movement trajectories, the perspectives of those with access to high-profile platforms, often journalists rather than movement participants, often present a soundbite skewed to gather clicks and shares. Instead, we have tried to demonstrate here that speaking to people about their motivations offers a valuable way of documenting social movements as they happen, with results that often diverge from the think pieces featured on the *Washington Post*'s Twitter feed. If, as the title of this section argues, a movement is its people, then social movement scholars must extend our focus to include everyday participants alongside movement leaders. By investing in the work of real-time movement documentation, rhetorical and media scholars can help to preserve a more accurate picture of the complexities, contradictions, and complications inherent in the struggle for social justice.

An added benefit, and one that in large part inspired this book, lies in the promotion of those social movements as important historical moments. It is difficult to predict what rhetorical and media scholars will be analyzing a century from today, but if they should look back at Memphis, Tennessee, in the 2010s, we believe BLM should be central to their understanding of the city's context. Documenting social movements as they happen allows scholars to promote important moments that might otherwise be overlooked based on ideological bias, arbitrary definitions of influence, or simple carelessness. We further urge scholars to uplift social movements locally, as our analysis of BLM and #ALM Memphis allowed us a more nuanced view of the politics at work. Social movement scholarship should include global and national perspectives to be sure, but an additional local focus allows us to uplift not only movements like BLM in general, but also the individual, everyday people who contributed to their national success. Neither BLM nor #ALM were monolithic, but the nuanced differences between participants are much more difficult to see and appreciate from a national or global perspective. We therefore urge scholars to take up local social movements, thereby uplifting their importance both at a large scale and in terms of everyday movement participants.

Second, we have emphasized context throughout this book, and we charge all of those taking up cultural analysis to similarly consider the ways historical context influences motivation at the individual level. Individual motivations and perspectives are built from contextual factors like economic stability (real and perceived), geographic location, personal networks, mediated and political representation, and others. All of these factors can be difficult to predict without talking to the people invested in them. Always at play in issues of context and motivation, history should be considered a primary context for any social movement analysis. Though the current political economy of academic publishing suggests that the new and different are of utmost importance, we find that most things carry traces of the past. Social media has new and different aspects, for example, but as we have demonstrated here, it has not reinvented our personal networks, nor does it deliver on the optimistic promise of a postracial utopia. Instead, social media allows for more efficient communication between social movement organizers, but is still very much reliant on personal networks, and users carry their "real life" histories into their social media interactions. The question of whether BLM is "your grandparents' movement" speaks to the reverberations of history in all things new. Just as BLM carries echoes of mid-twentieth-century civil rights organizing, #ALM reverberates with the same rhetorics present in historical countermovements. History is context, and both are forever central to understanding the present and future.

Historical context is not only important in terms of national and global history, but also in terms of personal, everyday, lived histories. Those who participate in social movements do so primarily based on their previously held beliefs and experiences. Their ideological perspectives permeate their online behaviors, on- and offline relationships, and the ways they interact with on-the-ground social action. Therefore, scholars of social movements must take into account the previous affiliations of movement participants. Religion, for example, proved to be a major factor in the ways our participants viewed BLM and #ALM, but we find that religion is not often discussed in critical social movement work. Speaking to the ways BLM deepened her own Christian faith, Brittney Cooper has noted that feminism, and we would add other social justice epistemologies, often rejects religion on the basis of its historical alignment with oppressive social structures.[8] Cooper argues:

> If I think feminism can change women's lives for the better, then I must work within church and faith spaces to offer alternate frameworks for women, rather than coming from the outside and saying, "God isn't real," and/or "Your God is patriarchal and sexist." That's only helpful in very limited circumstances. I'm deeply resistant to the idea that to be intellectual, or feminist, or woke, is to be anti-religion.[9]

As Cooper's comments indicate, and as our study further demonstrated, religious faith is not as simple as social movement scholars and leaders have often imagined. Following Cooper, we suggest that work in this area must consider religion as a complex context that is not necessarily predictive of a particular social justice stance, but instead that is deeply intertwined with the ways individuals understand and experience the world. As such, scholars and practitioners should look for ways of understanding previously held beliefs, including faith, in conversation with social justice ideals.

Finally, we are enthusiastic about the possibilities of social media for justice organizing, but we are simultaneously concerned with framings that neglect online communication's connection with material histories. Mid-twentieth-century civil rights organizing depended upon media technologies, ranging from Wide Area Telephone Service (WATS) lines to broadcast footage of events like Bloody Sunday. Leaders of these organizations knew that technology, as useful as it is, was insufficient for social change. These tools were most useful when they promoted and facilitated conversation among family, friends, coworkers, congregants, and other pre-existing social circles. At times, it seems we have transitioned from WATS and broadcast to Twitter and Facebook Live, but this book troubles this assumption in two ways. On one hand, we urge scholars and social leaders not to conceptualize older technologies as oppositional to their digital forms. By design, our participants were all engaged with online networking. Yet across the board, participants mentioned learning more about social issues through broadcast and cable television and radio. Just as footage from the Edmund Pettis bridge was dispersed through television airwaves, Facebook Live and other mobile video footage is often aired on local and national news stations. Social media often works alongside older technologies, not necessarily in opposition to them.

On the other, social media not only works with broadcast technologies; additionally, online networking works alongside traditional conversation circles. Throughout our interviews, participants wove their accounts of social media messaging together with their accounts of in-person conversation. This book suggests that, rather than being a replacement for traditional methods of movement organizing, social media works in ways similar to previous technologies; WATS, broadcast television, and radio programming were effective not because they replaced face-to-face conversation, but because they sparked and focused discussion between friends and acquaintances. Rather than imagining that contemporary social movements can lean on social media for recruitment, our results suggest that online social justice messaging may be better understood as a starting point for conversations. Social media users, in turn, can use the information they see online to discuss current issues and events, rather than assuming social justice messages begin and end on Twitter, Facebook, or other platforms.

To summarize the implications of this book, then, we urge scholars and practitioners to document and uplift social justice activity as it happens, to consider the contexts in which organizing happens, and to understand traditional and contemporary messaging platforms as complimentary rather than oppositional. In the case of BLM and #ALM in the greater Memphis area, at least, these factors featured prominently in making sense of a movement and a countermovement.

A CALL FOR JUSTICE

Throughout this book, we have demonstrated the sometimes predictable, sometimes surprising, but always powerful ways context influences individual motivations for or against social change. Our BLM-affiliated participants came to a social justice movement for a variety of reasons, and it is possible that some of our #ALM-affiliated participants might also be brought into the movement for Black lives. When we began this study, we did not anticipate our participants would have such a range of perspectives to share, or that the stories of how they came to identify with one group or the other (or both) would vary so dramatically. Of course, our initial assumptions were, like our participants, driven by context. Like most of our participants, a majority of our information about the "other group" had come from social and traditional media, often in the form of think pieces.[10] Perhaps we should not be surprised, then, that speaking with actual, everyday people resulted in a more diverse, nuanced picture of who affiliated with which group and why. In movements for justice and change, social media is only one tool. We believe it would be a mistake for anyone who hopes to make the world a more just place to neglect the value of both face-to-face, intimate conversation and on-the-ground action. To drive home this point, we conclude with a story that unites two historical contexts.

During the last year of Martin Luther King Jr.'s life, his ability to persuade and to gain a national consensus around issues of war, poverty, economic injustice, and the inequality suffered by African Americans and all people of color had waned. Faced with increasing hostility to him and the movement along with the rising white backlash that eventually would give birth to Nixon's silent majority coalition, King knew that moral suasion would not give him the results that he had hoped. Therefore, King began a campaign, grounded in non-violence, that aimed to force the government to act on behalf of the movement.

He planned to implement this strategy through the Poor People's Campaign. During a press conference on December 4, 1967,[11] Martin Luther King Jr. and members from the Southern Christian Leadership Council announced their plan to lead thousands of poor people—including all races, ethnicities, and nationalities—to the nation's capital to bring attention to the plight of people living in abject poverty. In announcing this major initiative, King stated,

> We will go there, we will demand to be heard, and we will stay until America responds. If this means forcible repression of our movement we will confront it, for we have done this before. If this means scorn or ridicule we embrace it, for that is what America's poor now receive. If it means jail we accept it willingly, for the millions of poor already are imprisoned by exploitation and discrimination.

King would further call for "dramatic expansion of nonviolent demonstrations in Washington and simultaneous protests elsewhere. In short, we will be petitioning our government for specific reforms and we intend to build militant nonviolent actions until that government moves against poverty."

Through all of this, King was clear that the campaign would not be a "mere one-day march." Instead, they would "stay until some definite and positive action is taken to provide jobs and income for the poor." The reason for this type of action, King argued, was that America was at a "crossroads of history and it is critically important for us as a nation and a society to choose a new path and move upon it with resolution and courage." For America to choose this new path, King argued that a new type of movement was needed:

> We have learned from hard and bitter experience in our movement that our government does not move to correct a problem involving race until it is confronted directly and dramatically. It required a Selma before the fundamental right to vote was written into the federal statutes. It took a Birmingham before the government moved to open doors of public accommodations to all human beings. What we now need is a new kind of Selma or Birmingham to dramatize the economic plight of the Negro and compel the government to act.

When a reporter mentioned that it seemed as if this new movement had a more militant tone to it, King responded:

> I would say that this will be a move that will be consciously designed to develop massive dislocation. I think this is absolutely necessary at this point. It will be massive dislocation without destroying life or property and we've found through our experience that timid supplications for justice will not solve the problem. We've got to massively confront the power structure. So this is a move to dramatize the situation, channelize the very legitimate and understandable rage of the ghetto and we know we can't do it with something weak. It has to be something strong, dramatic, and attention-getting.

No longer believing that government officials would "do the right thing," King called for a campaign of massive civil disobedience that would lead to economic boycotts and shut down entire cities. By doing this, King asked activists to bear witness[12] to their suffering in hopes that the action could convince the government to do the "right thing."

Of course, King did not live to see the Poor People's Campaign. He died by an assassin's bullet four months later. However, his call for massive disruption and dislocation has been heard from many activists. Almost fifty years later, on July 10, 2016, more than one thousand frustrated and fed up Memphis citizens took to the I-40 Bridge connecting Arkansas and Tennessee, in an act of mass civil disobedience to disrupt and shut down traffic.[13] These protesters were protesting the latest videos of the murders of Alton Sterling and Philando Castile that had gone viral, causing another round of trauma and pain in the minds and bodies of African Americans. While Sterling and Castile's murders were at the forefront of the protest, the atrocities and injustices that happen in Memphis on a daily basis electrified the air on the bridge. Calls for equal rights, economic justice, livable wage, fairer sentencing, crime reduction, and many others were heard on that day. However, what we found interesting is that many of those on the bridge that night had participated in our focus groups. As injustices continue to happen, we anticipate we will see more protest, spinning from social media into the street

As we write this, the #NeverAgain movement is in full force.[14] One of the things that activists in that movement have done with their notoriety is to bring attention to the gun violence that happens in inner city communities. Young, white Parkland students are actively engaging with predominately Black students from Chicago.[15] By engaging with other students and being open to listening to others who have also suffered at the hands of gun violence, they seek not to dominate the focus, but to expand the debate by bringing more voices to the public arena. Additionally, while they do this, they too learn about others who have been in this fight, and they become part of the much larger history of the movement. They pick up the baton of justice passed from the million of others throughout history who at first were vilified for their stands but now take their places on the right side of history. Contemporary justice moments may start on social media, but movements still happen in the street, in conversation, and in dialogue. The key to all lies in listening to the other and in believing their truth.

NOTES

1. Frances Robles and Jose A. Del Real, "Stephon Clark Was Shot 8 Times Primarily in His Back, Family-Ordered Autopsy Finds," *New York Times*, March 30, 2018, https://www.nytimes.com/2018/03/30/us/stephon-clark-independent-autopsy.html; Josiah Bates, "The Death of Stephon Clark: What We Know about the Sacramento Police Shooting," *ABC News*, March 29, 2018, http://abcnews.go.com/US/death-stephon-clark-police-shooting/story?id=54039443.

2. Nicole Chavez, "Body Camera Shows Officer Threatened to Shoot Alton Sterling within Seconds," *CNN*, March 31, 2018, https://www.cnn.com/2018/03/31/us/alton-sterling-police-videos-hearings/index.html.

3. Stuart Hall, "Encoding/Decoding," in Stuart Hall, Dorothy Hobson, Andrew Lowe, and Paul Willis (Eds.), *Culture, Media, Language* (London: Hutchinson, 1980), 128–39.

4. Andre E. Johnson and Anthony J. Stone, Jr., "'The Most Dangerous Negro in America': Rhetoric, Race and the Prophetic Pessimism of Martin Luther King, Jr.," *Journal of Communication and Religion* 21, no. 1 (2018): 9.

5. The Movement for Black Lives, "Platform. A Vision for Black Lives," retrieved from https://policy.m4bl.org/platform/.

6. Martin J. Medhurst, "The Contemporary Study of Public Address: Renewal, Recovery, and Reconfiguration," *Rhetoric and Public Affairs* 4, no. 3 (2000): 507.

7. Ibid.

8. Brittney Cooper, Interview by Janell Hobson, *Ms. Magazine*, February 19, 2018, http://msmagazine.com/blog/2018/02/19/interview-with-brittney-cooper/.

9. Ibid.

10. We both identify with BLM.

11. Press Conference Announcing the Poor People's Campaign, https://swap.stanford.edu/20141218232253/http://mlk-kpp01.stanford.edu/kingweb/publications/papers/unpub/671204–003_Announcing_Poor_Peoples_campaign.htm.

12. What we mean by "bearing witness" is to communicate a truth that sometimes is hard to communicate. Typically, when one bears witness, one is declaring that change may not happen soon or ever, but someone must stand watch and give an account of what happened. Many times, this bearing witness takes on a public stance, and just like many of the biblical prophets found in the Hebrew Bible, many of these accounts are performative in nature.

13. Wendi Thomas, "Take It to the Bridge," *#MLK50: Justice through Journalism*, July 7, 2017, https://mlk50.com/july-10–2016-take-it-to-the-bridge-e13744c16c21.

14. Emily Witt, "Urgency and Frustration: The Never Again Movement Gathers Momentum," *New Yorker*, February 23, 2018, https://www.newyorker.com/news/news-desk/urgency-and-frustration-the-never-again-movement-gathers-momentum.

15. Rachel Hinton, "Parkland Shooting Survivors Visit CPS Students to Plan Chicago Gun Control March," *Chicago Sun Times*, March 17, 2018, https://chicago.suntimes.com/chicago-politics/parkland-shooting-survivors-visit-cps-students-to-plan-chicago-gun-control-march/.

References

Ahmed, Sara. *The Cultural Politics of Emotion*. New York: Routledge, 2004.

Alexis, Diamond. "Chilli Responds to 'All Lives Matter' Backlash." *BET*, May 10, 2017. https://www.bet.com/music/2017/05/10/tlc-chilli-all-lives-matter.html.

Asen, Robert. "Ideology, Materiality, and Counterpublicity: William E. Simon and the Rise of a Conservative Counterintelligentsia." *Quarterly Journal of Speech* 95, no. 3 (2009): 263–88.

Ash, Stephen V. *Massacre in Memphis: The Race Riot That Shook the Nation One Year after the Civil War*. New York: Hill and Wang, 2013.

Bailey, Julius and David J. Leonard. "Black Lives Matter: Post-Nihilistic Freedom Dreams." *Journal of Contemporary Rhetoric* 5, no. 3, 4 (2015): 67–77.

Banet-Weiser, Sarah. *Authentic^{TM}: The Politics of Ambivalence in a Brand Culture*. New York: New York University Press, 2012.

Banks, Adelle. "Black Churches Are No Longer Ground Zero for Civil Rights Activism." *Religion News Service*, December 18, 2014. https://www.religionnews.com/2014/12/18/Black-churches-no-longer-ground-zero-civil-rights-activism/.

Barna Group. "Black Lives Matter and Racial Tension in America." Accessed March 25, 2018. https://www.barna.com/research/Black-lives-matter-and-racial-tension-in-america/.

Bates, Josiah. "The Death of Stephon Clark: What We Know about the Sacramento Police Shooting." *ABC News*, March 29, 2018. http://abcnews.go.com/US/death-stephon-clark-police-shooting/story?id=54039443.

Berlant, Lauren. *The Female Complaint: The Unfinished Business of Sentimentality in American Culture*. Durham, NC: Duke University Press, 2008.

Black Lives Matter and Alicia Garza. "Equal Justice Society." Accessed March 25, 2018. https://equaljusticesociety.org/Blacklivesmatter/.

Black Lives Matter. Official website. Accessed March 25, 2018. https://Blacklivesmatter.com/.

Black Lives Matter Memphis. "About: #BlackLivesMatter Memphis Chapter." Accessed March 25, 2018. https://Blacklivesmattermemphis.wordpress.com/about/.

Blake, John. "Is Black Lives Matter Blowing It?" *CNN*, August 2, 2016. https://www.cnn.com/2016/07/29/us/Black-lives-matter-blowing-it/index.html.

Bond, Julian and Elizabeth Gritter. "Interview with Julian Bond." *Southern Cultures* 12, no. 1 (2006). http://www.southerncultures.org/article/interview-julian-bond/.

Bonilla, Yarimar and Jonathan Rosa. "#Ferguson: Digital Protest, Hashtag Ethnography, and the Racial Politics of Social Media in the United States." *American Ethnologist* 42, no. 1 (2015): 4–17.

Bonilla-Silva, Eduardo. *Racism without Racists: Color-Blind Racism and Racial Inequality in Contemporary America*. Lanham, MD: Rowman & Littlefield, 2010.

Bradley, Anthony Bradley. "Black Lives Matter Doesn't Represent the Gospel, Nor Should It." *World*, January 15, 2016. https://world.wng.org/2016/01/Black_lives_matter_doesnt_represent_the_gospel_nor_should_it.

Bruns, Axel and Jean Burgess. "The Use of Twitter Hashtags in the Formation of Ad Hoc Publics." Paper presented at the European Consortium for Political Research conference, Reykjavik (August 25–27, 2011). https://eprints.qut.edu.au/46515/.

Calafell, Bernadette Marie and Dawn Marie MacIntosh. "Latina/o Vernacular Discourse: Theorizing Performative Dimensions of an Other Counterpublic." In *What Democracy Looks Like: The Rhetoric of Social Movements and Counterpublics*, edited by Christina R. Foust, Amy Pason, and Kate Rogness Zittlow, 201–24. Tuscaloosa: University of Alabama Press, 2017.

Carney, Nikita. "All Lives Matter, but So Does Race: Black Lives Matter and the Evolving Role of Social Media." *Humanity and Society* 40, no. 2 (2016): 180–99. https://doi.org/10.1177/0160597616643868.

Cathcart, Robert S. "A Confrontation Perspective on the Study of Social Movements." *Central States Speech Journal* 34, no. 1 (1983): 69–74.

Chavez, Nicole. "Body Camera Shows Officer Threatened to Shoot Alton Sterling within Seconds." *CNN*, March 31, 2018. https://www.cnn.com/2018/03/31/us/alton-sterling-police-videos-hearings/index.html.

Chessum, Jake. "Oprah Winfrey's Comments about Recent Protests and Ferguson Spark Controversy. *People*, January 1, 2015. http://people.com/celebrity/oprah-on-recent-protests-and-ferguson.

Chistakis, Erika. "My Halloween Email Led to a Campus Firestorm—and a Troubling Lesson about Self-Censorship." *Washington Post*, October 28, 2016. https://www.washingtonpost.com/opinions/my-halloween-email-led-to-a-campus-firestorm--and-a-troubling-lesson-about-self-censorship/2016/10/28/70e55732-9b97-11e6-a0ed-ab0774c1eaa5_story.html?utm_term=.e9088b7cc6b1.

Clark, Heather. "Christians Warn Upcoming Shack Movie Depicting God as Woman Could 'Far Outweigh' Harm of Novel." *Christian News*, December 20, 2016. http://christiannews.net/2016/12/20/christians-warn-upcoming-shack-movie-depicting-god-as-woman-could-far-outweigh-harm-of-novel/.

Cone, James. *Black Theology and Black Power.* NY: Seabury Press, 1969.

———. *The Cross and Lynching Tree.* Maryknoll, NY: Orbis Books, 2011.

Conversi, Daniele. "Irresponsible Radicalization: Diasporas, Globalization and Long-Distance Nationalism in the Digital Age." *Journal of Ethnic and Migration Studies* 38, no. 9 (2012): 1357–79. https://doi.org/10.1080/1369183X.2012.698204

Cooper, Brittney. "'Post-Racial America' Is a Dangerous Lie: Why the Fantasy Is Naive, Insidious and Deadly." *Salon.com*, February 25, 2014. http://www.salon.com/2014/02/25/stop_the_post_racial_fantasy_why_false_optimism_on_race_is_insidious_and_deadly/.

———. "Intersectionality." In *The Oxford Handbook of Feminist Theory*, edited by Lisa Disch and Mary Hakwesworth, 385–406. Oxford: Oxford University Press, 2016.

Corrigan, Lisa M. *Prison Power*. Jackson: University of Mississippi Press, 2017.

Crenshaw, Kimberle. "Demarginalizing the Intersection of Race and Sex: A Black Feminist Critique of Antidiscrimination Doctrine, Feminist Theory and Antiracist Politics." *University of Chicago Legal Forum* 1 (1989): 139–67.

Crowley, Ryan M. "Transgressive and Negotiated White Racial Knowledge." *International Journal of Qualitative Studies in Education* 29, no. 8 (2016): 1016–29.

Damiani, Jesse. "Every Time You Say 'All Lives Matter' You Are Being an Accidental Racist." *Huffington Post*, July 15, 2016. http://www.huffingtonpost.com/jesse-damiani/every-time-you-say-all-li_1_b_11004780.html.

Daniels, Jessie. "Race and Racism in Internet Studies: A Review and Critique." *New Media and Society* 15, no. 5 (2012): 695–719. https://doi.org/10.1177/1461444812462849.

David M. Rubenstein Gallery, National Archives. "Calls for Racial Justice Silenced 1917." Accessed March 25, 2018. http://recordsofrights.org/events/70/calls-for-racial-justice-silenced.

————. "The Loyalty of the American Negro." Accessed March 25, 2018. http://recordsofrights.org/records/189/the-loyalty-of-the-american-negro/1.

Day, Elizabeth. "#BlackLivesMatter: The Birth of a New Civil Rights Movement." *The Guardian*, July 19, 2015. https://www.theguardian.com/world/2015/jul/19/Blacklivesmatter-birth-civil-rights-movement.

DiAngelo, Robin. "White Fragility." *International Journal of Critical Pedagogy* 3, no. 3 (2011): 54–70.

DiAngelo, Robin and Özlem Sensoy. "Getting Slammed: White Depictions of Race Discussions as Arenas of Violence." *Race Ethnicity and Education* 17, no. 1 (2014): 103–28. https://doi.org/10.1080/13613324.2012.674023.

Dixon, Brandon. "A Broken Frame: Black Lives Matter." *Harvard Political Review*, May 22, 2016. http://harvardpolitics.com/covers/48277/.

Dixon, Kitsy. "Feminist Online Identity: Analyzing the Presence of Hashtag Feminism." *Journal of Arts and Humanities* 3, no. 7 (2014): 34–40.

Dyson, Michael Eric. *Can You Hear Me Now?: The Inspiration, Wisdom, and Insight of Michael Eric Dyson*. New York: Basic Books, 2009.

Edwards, Elise. "'Let's Imagine Something Different': Spiritual Principles in Contemporary African American Justice Movements and Their Implications for the Built Environment." *Religions* 8, no. 12 (2017): 2–22. https://doi.org/10.3390/rel8120256.

Elitou, Tweety. "This Artist Painted God as a Black Woman and Got a Lot of People Mad." *BET*, May 24, 2017. https://www.bet.com/style/2017/05/24/artist-goes-viral-with-black-woman-god.html.

Ellis, Mark. "'Closing Ranks' and 'Seeking Honors': W. E. B. Du Bois in World War I." *The Journal of American History* 79, no. 1 (1992): 96–124.

Equal Justice Initiative. "Resistance to Civil Rights." Accessed March 25, 2018. https://eji.org/racial-justice/resistance-civil-rights.

Farrag, Hebah H. "The Role of Spirit in the #BlackLivesMatter Movement: A Conversation with Activist and Artist Patrisse Cullors." *Religion Dispatches*, June 24, 2015. http://religiondispatches.org/the-role-of-spirit-in-the-Blacklivesmatter-movement-a-conversation-with-activist-and-artist-patrisse-cullors/.

Feagin, Joe R., Hernán Vera, and Pinar Batur. *White Racism: The Basics*. New York: Routledge, 1995.

Feminist Killjoys. "Selfcare as Warfare." *Feminist Killjoys*, August 25, 2014. https://feminist-killjoys.com/2014/08/25/selfcare-as-warfare/.

Flynn, Joseph E. Jr. "White Fatigue: Naming the Challenge in Moving from an Individual to a Systemic Understanding of Racism." *Multicultural Perspectives* 17, no. 3 (2015): 115–24.

Forman, Tyrone A. "Color-Blind Racism and Racial Indifference: The Role of Racial Apathy in Facilitating Enduring Inequalities." In *The Changing Terrain of Race and Ethnicity*, edited by Maria Krysan and Amanda E. Lewis, 43–66. New York: Russel Sage Foundation, 2004.

Freedan, Michael. "Editorial: Emotions, Ideology and Politics." *Journal of Political Ideologies* 18, no. 1 (2013): 1–10.

Furedi, Frank. *Culture of Fear Revisited*. London: Continuum, 2006.

Gallagher, Victoria J. and Kenneth S. Zagacki. "Visibility and Rhetoric: Epiphanies and Transformations in the Life Photographs of the Selma Marches of 1965." *Rhetoric Society Quarterly* 37, no. 2 (2007): 113–35.

Gay, Geneva and Kipchonge N. Kirkland. "Developing Cultural Critical Consciousness and Self-Reflection in Preservice Teacher Education." *Theory into Practice* 42, no. 3 (2003): 181–87.

Gil, Marta. "Emotions and Political Rhetoric: Perception of Danger, Group Conflict and the Biopolitics of Fear." *Human Affairs* 26, no. 2 (2016): 212–26. https://doi.org/10.1515/humaff-2016-0020.

Giroux, Henry A. *The Abandoned Generation: Democracy beyond the Culture of Fear*. New York: Palgrave MacMillan, 2003.

Gladwell, Malcolm. "Does Egypt Need Twitter? New Yorker Political Scene Blog." *New Yorker*, February 2, 2011. https://www.newyorker.com/news/news-desk/does-egypt-need-twitter.

Goodman, Steve. *Sonic Warfare: Sound, Affect, and the Ecology of Fear*. Cambridge, MA: The MIT Press, 2010.

Goudsouzian, Aram and Charles W. McKinney, Jr. "Introduction." In *An Unseen Light: Black Struggles for Freedom in Memphis, Tennessee*, edited by Aram Goudsouzian and Charles W. McKinney, Jr., 1–12. Lexington, KY: University Press of Kentucky, 2018.

Green, Emma. "Black Activism, Unchurched." *The Atlantic*, March 22, 2016. https://www.theatlantic.com/politics/archive/2016/03/Black-activism-baltimore-Black-church/474822/.

Greenberg, Alissa. "What the Woman Who Invented the Term 'White Fragility' Thinks about Trump." *The Stranger*, April 5, 2017. https://www.thestranger.com/features/2017/04/05/25056620/what-the-woman-who-invented-the-term-white-fragility-thinks-about-trump.

Gring-Pemble, Lisa M. "'It's We the People . . . , Not We the Illegals': Extreme Speech in Prince William County, Virginia's Immigration Debate." *Communication Quarterly* 60, no. 5 (2012): 624–48.

Gunn, Joshua. "On Speech and Public Release." *Rhetoric and Public Affairs* 13, no. 2 (2010): 1–41.

Gunning Francis, Leah. *Ferguson and Faith: Sparking Leadership and Awakening Community*. St. Louis: Chalice Press, 2015.

Hall, Stuart. "Encoding/Decoding." In *Culture, Media, Language*, edited by Stuart Hall, Dorothy Hobson, Andrew Lowe, and Paul Willis, 128–139. London: Hutchinson, 1980.

Hensman Kettrey, Heather and Whitney Nicole Laster. "Staking Territory in the 'World White Web': An Exploration of the Roles of Overt and Color-Blind Racism in Maintaining Racial Boundaries on a Popular Web Site." *Social Currents* 1, no. 3 (2014): 257–74.

Hill, Theon. "Sanitizing the Struggle: Barack Obama, Selma, and Civil Rights Memory." *Communication Quarterly* 65, no. 3 (2017): 354–76.

Hill Collins, Patricia. *Black Sexual Politics: African Americans, Gender, and the New Racism*. New York: Routledge, 2004.

Hinton, Rachel. "Parkland Shooting Survivors Visit CPS Students to Plan Chicago Gun Control March." *Chicago Sun Times*, March 17, 2018. https://chicago.suntimes.com/chicago-politics/parkland-shooting-survivors-visit-cps-students-to-plan-chicago-gun-control-march/.

Hobson, Janelle. "Interview with Brittney Cooper." *Ms. Magazine*, February 19, 2018. http://msmagazine.com/blog/2018/02/19/interview-with-brittney-cooper/.

Hoerl, Kristen. "Burning Mississippi into Memory? Cinematic Amnesia as a Resource for Remembering Civil Rights." *Critical Studies in Media Communication* 26, no. 1 (2009): 54–79.

Hoerl, Kristen and Erin Ortiz. "Organizational Secrecy and the FBI's COINTELPRO–Black Nationalist Hate Groups Program, 1967–1971." *Management Communication Quarterly* 29 (2015): 590–615.

hooks, bell. *Black Looks: Race and Representation*. New York: South End Press, 1992.

Hopkins, Peter E. and Susan J. Smith. "Scaling Segregation; Racializing Fear." In *Fear: Critical Geopolitics and Everyday Life*, edited by Rachel Pain and Susan J. Smith, 103–16. Aldershot, NH: Ashgate Publishing Limited, 2010.

Horne, Florian. "Prophetic Witness in the News and as News." *Media Development* 59, no. 1 (2012): 57–60.

House, Christopher A. "Crying for Justice: The #BLACKLIVESMATTER Religious Rhetoric of Bishop T.D. Jakes." *Southern Journal of Communication* 83, no. 1 (2018): 13–27. https://doi.org/10.1080/1041794X.2017.1387600.

Hughes, Robin L. and Natasha Flowers. "Colonizing Black Lives: The 'Crusade' for All Lives and White Fragility." *Diverse: Issues in Higher Education*, January 31, 2016. http://diverseeducation.com/article/80792/.

Jackson, Jenn. "Doing the Work: White People Must Invest in Anti-Racism." *Bitch Media*, December 26, 2017. https://www.bitchmedia.org/article/white-people-invest-in-anti-racism.

Jackson, Sarah J. "(Re)imagining Intersectional Democracy from Black Feminism to Hashtag Activism." *Women's Studies in Communication* 39, no. 4 (2016): 375–79.

Jayakumar, Uma M. and Annie S. Adamian. "The Fifth Frame of Colorblind Ideology: Maintaining the Comforts of Colorblindness in the Context of White Fragility." *Sociological Perspectives* 60, no. 5 (2017): 912–36. https://doi.org/10.1177/0731121417721910

Johnson, Andre E. "God Is a Negro: The (Rhetorical) Black Theology of Bishop Henry McNeal Turner." *Black Theology: An International Journal* 13, no. 1 (April 2015): 29–40. https://doi.org/10.1179/1476994815Z.00000000045.

———. "Teaching in Ferguson: A Rhetorical Autoethnography from a Scholar/Activist." *Southern Communication Journal* 81, no. 4 (2016): 267–69. https://doi.org/10.1080/1041794X.2016.1200126.

———. "The Fallacy of Racial Reconciliation." *Rhetoric, Race, and Religion Blog*, March 16, 2018. http://www.patheos.com/blogs/rhetoricraceandreligion/2018/03/fallacy-racial-reconciliation.html.

———. "'To Make the World So Damn Uncomfortable': W. E. B. Du Bois and the African American Prophetic Tradition." *Carolinas Communication Annual* 32 (2016): 16–29.

———. "The Prophetic Persona of James Cone and the Rhetorical Theology of Black Theology." *Black Theology Journal* 8, no. 3 (2010): 266–85.

Johnson, Andre E. and Anthony J. Stone, Jr. "'The Most Dangerous Negro in America': Rhetoric, Race and the Prophetic Pessimism of Martin Luther King, Jr." *Journal of Communication and Religion* 21, no. 1 (2018): 8–22.

Johnson, Wray R. "Black American Radicalism and the First World War: The Secret Files of the Military Intelligence Division." *Armed Forces and Society* 26, no. 1 (1999): 27–53. https://doi.org/10.1177/0095327X9902600103.

Jones, Robert P., Daniel Cox, Betsy Cooper, and Rachel Lienesch. "Anxiety, Nostalgia, and Mistrust: Findings from the 2015 America Values Survey." *Public Religion Research Institute*, November 17, 2015. https://www.prri.org/wp-content/uploads/2015/11/PRRI-AVS-2015.pdf.

Jordan, Jason. "We'll Have No Race Trouble Here: Racial Politics and Memphis' Reign of Terror." In *An Unseen Light: Black Struggles for Freedom in Memphis, Tennessee*, edited by Aram Goudsouzian and Charles W. McKinney, Jr., 130–49. Lexington, KY: University Press of Kentucky, 2018.

Juris, Jeffrey S. "Reflections on #Occupy Everywhere: Social Media, Public Space, and Emerging Logics of Aggregation." *American Ethnologist* 39, no. 2 (2012): 259–79.

Kassian, Mary. "Re-imagining God in the Shack." *The Council on Biblical Manhood and Womanhood*, April 17, 2009. https://cbmw.org/uncategorized/re-imagining-god-in-the-shack/.

Kennedy, Randall. "The Civil Rights Movement and the Politics of Memory." *American Prospect*, May 12, 2015. http://prospect.org/article/civil-rights-movement-and-politics-memory.

Kinchen, Shirletta J. *Black Power in the Bluff City: African American Youth and Student Activism in Memphis, 1965–1975.* Knoxville: University of Tennessee Press, 2016.

King, Martin Luther, Jr. "I've Been to the Mountaintop." *American Rhetoric*, April 3, 1968. http://www.americanrhetoric.com/speeches/mlkivebeentothemountaintop.htm.

Kirabo, Sincere. "Why White America Demonizes the #BlackLivesMatter Movement—And Why That Must Change." *The Establishment*, February 18, 2017. https://theestablishment.co/why-white-america-demonizes-the-Blacklivesmatter-movement-and-why-that-must-change-4cda83727063.

Klein, Naomi. "Occupy Wall Street: The Most Important Thing in the World Now." *Critical Quarterly* 54, no. 2 (2012): 1–4.

Kwon, K. Hazel, Shin-Il Moon, and Michael A. Stefanone. "Unspeaking on Facebook? Testing Network Effects on Self-Censorship of Political Expressions in Social Network Sites." *Quality and Quantity* 49, no. 4 (2016): 1417–35.

Laneri, Raquel. "Uproar over Artist's Painting of God as a Black Woman." *New York Post*, May 30, 2017. https://nypost.com/2017/05/30/uproar-over-artists-painting-of-god-as-a-Black-woman/.

Leading the Way. "Six Major Problems with *The Shack.*" *Leading the Way*, February 24, 2017. http://www.ltw.org/read/articles/2017/03/six-major-problems-with-the-shack.

Lebron, Christopher. *The Making of Black Lives Matter: A Brief History of an Idea*. New York: Oxford University Press, 2017.

Lee, Murray. "The Enumeration of Anxiety: Power, Knowledge and Fear of Crime." In *Fear of Crime: Critical Voices in an Age of Anxiety*, edited by Stephen Farral and Murray Lee, 32–44. New York: Routledge, 2008.

Leff, Michael C. "The Habitation of Rhetoric." In *Rethinking Rhetorical Theory, Criticism, and Pedagogy*, edited by Antonio de Velasco, John Angus Campbell, and David Henry. East Lansing: Michigan State University Press, 2016, 143–62.

Leurs, Koen. "Digital Passages: Moroccan-Dutch Youths Performing Diaspora, Gender and Youth Cultural Identities across Digital Space." PhD diss., Utrecht University, 2012.

Linder, Chris. "Navigating Guilt, Shame, and Fear of Appearing Racist: A Conceptual Model of Antiracist White Feminist Identity Development." *Journal of College Student Development* 56, no. 6 (2015): 535–50.

Lotz, Amanda. "Assessing Qualitative Television Audience Research: Incorporating Feminist and Anthropological Theoretical Innovation." *Communication Theory* 10, no. 4 (2000): 447–67. https://doi.org/10.1111/j.1468-2885.2000.tb00202.x.

Mackin, Glenn. "Black Lives Matter and the Concept of the Counterworld." *Philosophy and Rhetoric* 49, no. 4 (2016): 459–81.

Maddux, Kristy. "When Patriots Protest: The Anti-Suffrage Discursive Transformation of 1917." *Rhetoric and Public Affairs* 7, no. 3 (2004): 283–310.

Matias, Cheryl E. "'And Our Feelings Just Don't Feel It Anymore': Re-Feeling Whiteness, Resistance, and Emotionality." *Understanding and Dismantling Privilege* 4, no. 2 (2014): 134–53. http://www.wpcjournal.com/article/view/12176/pdf_2.

———. "'Why Do You Make Me Hate Myself?': Re-Teaching Whiteness, Abuse, and Love in Urban Teacher Education." *Teaching Education* 27, no. 2 (2016): 194–211. https://doi.org/10.1080/10476210.2015.1068749.

McClain, Dani. "What Does Black Lives Matter Want? Now Its Demands Are Clearer Than Ever." *The Nation*, August 1, 2016. https://www.thenation.com/article/what-does-Black-lives-matter-want-we-now-have-it-in-writing/.

McIlwain, Charlton, Deen Freelon, and Meredith Clark. "Beyond the Hashtags: #Ferguson, #Blacklivesmatter, and the Online Struggle for Offline Justice." *Center for Media and Social Impact*, February 29, 2016. http://cmsimpact.org/resource/beyond-hashtags-ferguson-Blacklivesmatter-online-struggle-offline-justice/.

Medhurst, Martin J. "The Contemporary Study of Public Address: Renewal, Recovery, and Reconfiguration." *Rhetoric and Public Affairs* 4, no. 3 (2000): 495–511.

Mendez, Xhercis. "Which Black Lives Matter?" *Radical History Review* 126 (October 2016): 96–105.

Mercieca, Jennifer Rose. "The Culture of Honor: How Slaveholders Responded to the Abolitionist Mail Crisis of 1835." *Rhetoric and Public Affairs* 10, no. 1 (2007): 51–76.

Meyer, David S. and Suzanne Staggenborg. "Movements, Countermovements, and the Structure of Political Opportunity." *American Journal of Sociology* 101, no. 6 (1996): 1628–60.

Middleton, Michael, Aaron Hess, Danielle Endres, and Samatha Senda-Cook. *Critical Participatory Rhetoric: Theoretical and Methodological Foundations for Studying Rhetoric in Situ*. Lanham, MD: Lexington Books, 2015.

Mirk, Sarah. "Audre Lorde Thought of Self-Care as an 'Act of Political Warfare.'" *Bitch Media*, February 18, 2016. https://www.bitchmedia.org/article/audre-lorde-thought-self-care-act-political-warfare.

Morrissey, Megan E. and Christy-Dale L. Sims. "Playing the Race Card: Antiracial Bordering and Rhetorical Practices of New Racism." *The Review of Communication* 15, no. 2 (2015): 81–101.

Moss, Christina. "A Time to Remember: Rhetoric, Commemoration and Activism." In *Activism and Rhetoric: Theories and Contexts for Political Engagement*, edited by JongHwa Lee and Seth Kahn. New York: Routledge, 2018.

Mottl, Tahi L. "An Analysis of Countermovements." *Social Problems* 27, no. 5 (1980): 620–35.

Nakamura, Lisa. *Digitizing Race: Visual Culture of the Internet*. Minneapolis: University of Minnesota Press, 2008.

Nakamura, Lisa and Peter Chow-White. *Race after the Internet*. New York: Routledge, 2012.

New York Times Editorial Board. "The Truth of 'Black Lives Matter.'" *New York Times*, September 3, 2015. https://www.nytimes.com/2015/09/04/opinion/the-truth-of-black-lives-matter.html.

Nicol, Val. *Social Economies of Fear and Desire: Emotional Regulation, Emotion Management, and Embodied Autonomy*. New York: Palgrave MacMillan, 2011.

Oliver, Kelly. *Witnessing: Beyond Recognition*. Minneapolis: University of Minnesota Press, 2001.

Ono, Kent. "Postracism: A Theory of the 'Post' as Political Strategy." *Journal of Communication Inquiry* 34, no. 3, (2010): 227–33.

Orbe, Mark. "#AllLivesMatter as Post-Racial Rhetorical Strategy." *Journal of Contemporary Rhetoric* 5, no. 3/4 (2015): 90–98.

———. *Communication Realities in a "Post-Racial" Society: What the U.S. Public Really Thinks of President Barack Obama*. Lanham, MD: Lexington Books, 2011.

Orozco, Richard and Jesus Jaime Diaz. "'Suited to Their Needs': White Innocence as a Vestige of Segregation." *Multicultural Perspectives* 18, no. 3 (2016): 127–33.

Pittman, Taylor. "Matt McGorry Calls Out Piers Morgan's Absurd Queen Bey Critique." *Huffington Post*, April 26, 2016. https://www.huffingtonpost.com/entry/matt-mcgorry-calls-out-piers-morgans-absurd-queen-bey-critique_us_571f74f2e4b01a5ebde33e66.

Postill, John and Sarah Pink. "Social Media Ethnography: The Digital Researcher in a Messy Web." *Media International Australia* 145 (2012): 123–34.

Public Enemy. "Louder Than a Bomb." June 28, 1988, Chung King Studios and Greene St. Recording in Manhattan, Sabella Studios in Long Island. Track 7, *It Takes a Nation of Millions to Hold Us Back*, 1988, cassette.

Reddick, Krystal. "Self-Care as Revolutionary Action." *Huffington Post*, January 6, 2015. https://www.huffingtonpost.com/krystal-reddick/selfcare-as-revolutionary_b_6393154.html.

Reiss, Steven. "Multifaceted Nature of Intrinsic Motivation: The Theory of 16 Basic Desires." *Review of General Psychology* 8 (2004): 179–93.

Reynolds, Barbara. "I Was a Civil Rights Activist in the 1960s. But It's Hard for Me to Get behind Black Lives Matter." *Washington Post*, August 24, 2015. https://www.washingtonpost.com/posteverything/wp/2015/08/24/i-was-a-civil-rights-activist-in-the-1960s-but-its-hard-for-me-to-get-behind-Black-lives-matter/?utm_term=.8b9fb3b49d3f.

Rightler-McDaniels, Jodi L. and Elizabeth M. Hendrickson. "Hoes and Hashtags: Constructions of Gender and Race in Trending Topics." *Social Semiotics* 24, no. 2 (2014): 175–90.

Robinson, Lisa. "Some Honest Thoughts on #BlackLivesMatter, the Church and Real Reconciliation." *Lisa Robinson: Thinking and Living Theological Thoughts Out Loud*, May 13, 2016. https://theothoughts.com/2016/05/13/some-honest-thoughts-on-Blacklivesmatter-the-church-and-real-reconciliation/.

Robles, Frances and Jose A. Del Real. "Stephon Clark Was Shot 8 Times Primarily in His Back, Family-Ordered Autopsy Finds." *New York Times*, March 30, 2018. https://www.nytimes.com/2018/03/30/us/stephon-clark-independent-autopsy.html.

Rost, Katja, Lea Stahel, and Bruno S. Frey. "Digital Social Norm Enforcement: Online Firestorms in Social Media." *PLoS One* 11, no. 6 (2016): 1–26. https://doi.org/10.1371/journal.pone.0155923.

Saltzman Chafetz, Janet and Anthony Gary Dworkin. "In the Face of Threat: Organized Antifeminism in Comparative Perspective." *Gender and Society* 1, no. 1 (1987): 33–60.

Sauter, Michael B., Evan Comen, and Samuel Stebbins. "16 Most Segregated Cities in America." *24/7 Wall Street*, July 21, 2017. https://247wallst.com/special-report/2017/07/21/16-most-segregated-cities-in-america/.

Sebastian, Simone. "Don't Criticize Black Lives Matter for Provoking Violence. The Civil Rights Movement Did, Too." *Washington Post*, October 1, 2015. https://

www.washingtonpost.com/posteverything/wp/2015/10/01/dont-criticize-Black-lives-mat-
ter-for-provoking-violence-the-civil-rights-movement-did-too/?utm_term=.ed2a1580eec6.

Sender, Katherine. *The Makeover: Reality Television and Reflexive Audiences.* New York: New York University Press, 2012.

Sharma, Sanjay. "Black Twitter? Racial Hashtags, Networks and Contagion," *New Formation* 78 (2013): 46–64.

Slater, Tom. "Black Lives Matter Has a Plantation Mentality." *Spiked*, October 19, 2016. http://www.spiked-online.com/newsite/article/Black-lives-matter-has-a-plantation-mentality-elaine-brown-Black-panthers/18888#.Wrj6PS7wZhF.

Sleeter, Christine. "White Silence, White Solidarity." In *Race Traitor*, edited by Noel Ignatiev and John Garvey, 257–67. New York: Routledge, 1996.

Small, Deborah. "Interview with Patrisse Khan-Cullors." *The Root*, January 8, 2018. https://www.theroot.com/Black-womens-lives-matter-a-discussion-with-blm-co-fou-1821866044.

Smith, Susan and Rachel Pain. "Critical Geopolitics and Everyday Fears." In *Fear of Crime: Critical Voices in an Age of Anxiety*, edited by Stephen Farrall and Murray Lee, 45–58. New York: Routledge, 2008.

Sproul, Emily. "The Missing Gospel in Black Lives Matter." *Baptist News*, September 23, 2016. https://baptistnews.com/article/the-missing-gospel-in-Black-lives-matter/.

Squires, Catherine, Eric King Watts, Mary Douglas Vavrus, Kent A. Ono, Kathleen Feyh, Bernadette Marie Calafell, and Daniel C. Brouwer. "What Is This 'Post-' in Postracial, Postfeminist . . . (Fill in the Blank?)." *Journal of Communication Inquiry* 34, no. 3 (2010): 210–53. https://doi.org/10.1177/0196859910371375.

Strauss, Anselm L. *Qualitative Analysis for Social Scientists.* Cambridge: Cambridge University Press, 1987.

Sweet, Madeleine. "'Separate but Equal,' #AllLivesMatter and Rewording the Reign of White Supremacy." *Huffington Post*, August 10, 2016. http://www.huffingtonpost.com/entry/separate-but-equal-alllivesmatter-and-rewording_us_57ab8e5ce4b091a07ef86347.

Tabachnick, Rachel. "The John Birch Society's Anti-Civil Rights Campaign of the 1960's and Its Relevance Today." *Political Research Associates*, January 21, 2014. http://www.politicalresearch.org/2014/01/21/the-john-birch-societys-anti-civil-rights-campaign-of-the-1960s-and-its-relevance-today/#sthash.hgyzLvr5.dpbs.

Tesfamariam, Rahiel. "Why the Modern Civil Rights Movement Keeps Religious Leaders at Arm's Length." *Washington Post*, September 18, 2015. https://www.washingtonpost.com/opinions/how-Black-activism-lost-its-religion/2015/09/18/2f56fc00-5d6b-11e5-8e9e-dce8a2a2a679_story.html?utm_term=.141dfb55b87f.

The Black Radical Congress. "A Black Freedom Agenda for the Twenty-First Century." *The Black Scholar* 28, no. 1 (1998): 71–73.

The Movement for Black Lives. "Platform. A Vision for Black Lives." Accessed March 25, 2018. https://policy.m4bl.org/platform/.

Thelwell, Ekwueme Michael. "Foreword." In *Die Nigger Die!* by H. Rap Brown, i–xxii. Chicago, IL: Lawrence Hill, 1969.

Thomas, Wendi. "Take It to the Bridge." *#MLK50: Justice through Journalism*, July 7, 2017. https://mlk50.com/july-10-2016-take-it-to-the-bridge-e13744c16c21.

Titley, Gavan. "No Apologies for Cross-Posting: European Trans-Media Space and the Digital Circuitries of Racism." *Crossings: Journal of Migration* 5, no. 1 (2014): 41–55. https://doi.org/10.1386/cjmc.5.1.41_1.

Townes, Carimah. "Obama Explains the Problem with 'All Lives Matter.'" *Think Progress*, October 22, 2015. https://thinkprogress.org/obama-explains-the-problem-with-all-lives-matter-780912d54888.

University of California Press. "The Black Panther Party's Ten-Point Program." Accessed March 25, 2018. https://www.ucpress.edu/blog/25139/the-Black-panther-partys-ten-point-program/.

Useem, Burt and Mayer N. Zald. "From Pressure Group to Social Movement: Organizational Dilemmas of the Effort to Promote Nuclear Power." *Social Problems* 30, no. 2 (1982): 144–56.

Vats, Anjali. "Cooking Up Hashtag Activism: #PaulasBestDishes and Counternarratives of Southern Food." *Communication and Critical/Cultural Studies* 12, no. 2 (2015): 209–13.

Warner, Benjamin R. "Modeling Partisan Media Effects in the 2014 U.S. Midterm Elections." *Journalism and Mass Media Quarterly* (2017). https://doi.org/10.1177/1077699017712991.

Wilkes, Andrew. "From Black Messiah to Black Lives Matter: How Pentecostal Piety Can Reveal the Charade of Racialized Capitalism." *The Guardian*, January 18, 2015. https://www.theguardian.com/commentisfree/2015/jan/18/black-messiah-black-lives-matter-pentecostal-piety-racialized-capitalism.

Williams, Thomas. "Saint Anselm." *Stanford Encyclopedia of Philosophy*. Accessed March 25, 2018. https://plato.stanford.edu/entries/anselm/#FaiSeeUndChaPurAnsThePro.

Wilson, Kirt. "Dreams of Union, Days of Conflict: Communicating Social Justice and Civil Rights Memory in the Age of Barack Obama." *National Communication Association*. Carroll C. Arnold Lecture, Philadelphia, 2016.

Wimbush, Vincent L. "Introduction: Interpreting Resistance, Resisting Interpretations." *Semeia* 79 (1997): 1–10.

Witt, Emily. "Urgency and Frustration: The Never Again Movement Gathers Momentum." *New Yorker*, February 23, 2018. https://www.newyorker.com/news/news-desk/urgency-and-frustration-the-never-again-movement-gathers-momentum.

WMC Action News 5 Staff. "City Hall Releases Updated 'Blacklist.'" *WMC Action News 5*, March 1, 2017. http://www.wmcactionnews5.com/story/34638607/names-added-to-city-hall-Blacklist-in-error-have-been-removed.

Wodak, Ruth. *The Politics of Fear: What Right-Wing Populist Discourses Mean*. London: Sage, 2015.

Wolf, Allison B. "'Tell Me How That Makes You Feel': Philosophy's Reason/Emotion Divide and Epistemic Pushback in Philosophy Classrooms." *Hypatia* 32, no. 4 (2017): 893–910. https://doi.org/10.1111/hypa.12378.

Young, Darrius. "The Saving of Black America's Body and White America's Soul: The Lynching of Ell Persons and the Rise of Black Activism in Memphis." In *An Unseen Light: Black Struggles for Freedom in Memphis, Tennessee*, edited by Aram Goudsouzian and Charles W. McKinney, Jr., 39–60. Lexington, KY: University Press of Kentucky, 2018.

Index

emotion, 26, 30, 33–34, 42

fear, 26, 27–28, 69–70, 71, 73–75, 76–79, 82–85, 89, 94–95, 100, 112

guilt, 27, 80–81

hate, 5, 78, 94, 106; shame, 69, 91–92. *See also* affect

Evangelical, 48, 56, 61, 62, 65

Ferguson, Missouri, xi, xiv–xv, 4, 6–7, 47, 52, 91, 92, 93. *See also* Brown, Michael (Mike)

Gaines, Korryn, 111
Garner, Eric, 111
Garza, Alicia, 6–7, 7–8, 50
Gray, Freddie, 111

internalized racism, 29
Intersectionality, 9, 13–14, 14–15, 28–29, 39–40, 49–50, 52–53

Jesus, 56, 58
journalism, xi, xii, xvii, 5–6, 10–11, 11–12, 12–13, 26–27, 28, 29–30, 36, 69–70, 80, 91, 93, 94, 114–115, 116–117, 118; Black journalism, xiii, 91

King, Martin Luther Jr., xiv, 1, 5, 14, 32–33, 35, 47, 52, 90, 91, 112–113, 118; Poor People's Campaign, xxi, 118–120; Sanitation Worker's Strike, xxi, 35; gay, 13–14, 14–15, 48; lesbian, 13–14, 14–15; transgender, 7, 13, 13–14, 89; queer, 13, 14, 39–40, 49–50

Lorde, Audre, 102, 104–105
Lyles, Charleena, 111

Malcolm X, 9, 90, 91, 112–113
Mandela, Nelson, 1–2
Martin, Trayvon, xi, 10–11, 12, 14, 30, 31, 111; Justice4Trayvon, xi; HoodiesUp, xi
Memphis, xiii–xiv, xviii, xx, 32–33, 34, 35, 36, 41, 54, 104, 115; Beale Street,

xiii, xxiv; bridge protest, 119–120; greensward movement, 9–10; LeMoyne-Owen College, xiv; Memphis Massacre, xiii, xxiv. *See also* Black Lives Matter (BLM Memphis); Crump, E. H. (Boss); Ell Persons; surveillance (Black List)
method, xvii; audience ethnography, xvii, xviii, 112–113, 114–116; autoethnography, 52; ethnography, xvii, xviii–xix, 69, 78–79; quantitative, xii, xix, 62–63; textual analysis, xvii, xxi, 111–112, 112–113, 114–115. *See also* rhetoric
millennial, 7–8, 16, 23
multiculturalism, 28, 72, 81

NAACP, xiii, xiii–xiv, 53–54, 91
neoliberalism, 36, 37, 71, 72–73, 73–74
#NeverAgain, 120
nonviolence, 1, 1–2, 4–5, 52, 92, 119

Obama, Barack, 70, 71–72, 73, 78; first Black president, 70, 71–72, 78
Occupy Wall Street, xv, xvi

Parkland, Florida (school shooting), 120
participatory critical rhetoric. *See* rhetoric
Pentecostal piety, 49, 51, 52, 53, 54, 57, 60, 65
Persons, Ell, xiii, xxiv
police xiii, 1–2, 3, 6, 10–11, 18, 30–32, 58, 62, 83–84, 90; harassment (brutality, violence), xiii–xiv, 6, 7, 9, 12, 23, 28, 30, 38–39, 73–74, 78–79, 79–80, 94, 98–99, 107, 111; Memphis Police Department, xiv, 57–58, 90. *See also* surveillance (Black List); Wilson, Darren
politics, xii, xv–xvi, xix, xxi, 3–4, 5, 12–13, 17, 26–27, 33, 62–63, 71–72, 91, 97–98, 99, 111, 113, 115–116; 2008 Presidential election, 69–70, 71, 73, 78, 99–100; 2016 Presidential election, xxi, 78; Democrats, 51, 71; GOP, 3–4, 36–37, 70, 71, 73, 91. *See also* Bush, George W.; Obama, Barack
Poor People's Campaign. *See* King, Martin Luther, Jr.

About the Authors

Amanda Nell Edgar is assistant professor of communication at the University of Memphis. Dr. Edgar's research explores the entanglement of sound and identity in popular culture. She is the author of *Culturally Speaking: The Rhetoric of Voice and Identity in a Mediated Culture* (forthcoming) and was the recipient of the Janice Hocker Rushing Early Career Research Award in 2018. Additionally, her work has appeared in *Quarterly Journal of Speech*, *Women's Studies in Communication*, *Communication and Critical/Cultural Studies*, and other journals, and has been featured on the National Communication Association's *Communication Currents.*

Andre E. Johnson is assistant professor of communication at the University of Memphis where he teaches classes in African American public address, rhetoric, race, and religion. Dr. Johnson is currently collecting the writings of nineteenth-century AME Bishop Henry McNeal Turner and directs the Digital Archive of the *Henry McNeal Turner Project*. He is also the author of *No Future in This Country: The Prophetic Pessimism of Bishop Henry McNeal Turner* (forthcoming), a rhetorical history of Turner's career from 1895–1915. Additionally, his work has appeared in the *Journal of Communication and Religion*, *Howard Journal of Communications*, *Southern Communication Journal*, and the *Journal of Contemporary Rhetoric.*

Made in the USA
Monee, IL
16 July 2020